Love, Relationships, and Society

Love, Relationships, and Society

One Thousand Quotes and Applications

≈

MUHAMMAD HASSAN RAZA

RESOURCE *Publications* · Eugene, Oregon

LOVE, RELATIONSHIPS, AND SOCIETY
One Thousand Quotes and Applications

Resource Publications
An Imprint of Wipf and Stock Publishers
199 W. 8th Ave., Suite 3
Eugene, OR 97401

www.wipfandstock.com

PAPERBACK ISBN: 979-8-3852-3963-4
HARDCOVER ISBN: 979-8-3852-3964-1
EBOOK ISBN: 979-8-3852-3965-8

For additional questions and resources, please directly contact the author at twosoulsonereflection@gmail.com

I dedicate this book to my family which is as follows:
Zeenat Raza (My wife)
Hussain Raza (My older son)
Rasti Raza (My daughter)
Ali Raza (My younger son)

Table of Contents

About the Author

DR. RAZA IS AN associate professor at Missouri State University, Springfield, United States. He is a theorist and a methodologist. He is the author of Two Souls One Reflection and The Multilevel Community Engagement Model: School, Community, and Workplace Engagement and Service-Learning. He has been writing poetry, songs, and quotes since he was in high school. He writes poetry in English and Urdu. In addition to writing poetry, songs, and quotes, he also writes dramas and films. After work, he likes to spend time with his family, which includes his spouse and three young children. He also likes to travel and visit new places to explore and enjoy.

About the Book

LOVE, RELATIONSHIPS, AND SOCIETY is the first book of its kind. There are two parts of this book. In the first part, there are forty chapters. Each chapter demonstrates the application of one unique quote. In the second part, there are one thousand quotes, which are also unique statements. These quotes have never been written or said in the past. The chapters contain forty quotes related to love, relationships, and society, which are written by the author. These quotes are unique statements of various kinds. These quotes provide readers with useful information on love, relationships, and society. The author also provides a description of each quote to further explain the information and make readers more familiar with each quote. Additionally, there is a story for each quote along with a moral to further demonstrate a real-life application of each quote. Readers can also write their own quote, a description, and a story related to each quote and actively engage themselves in this book. The author also provides a brief introduction to each chapter.

Moreover, a description of an activity that further fosters readers' engagement and promotes a real-life application of the quote is provided. This activity takes readers beyond the classroom or any formal setting and engages them with those groups who are outside formal settings but have unique real-life experiences to share related to the topic. The author also provides discussion questions that are informed by the quote. These questions promote critical thinking, group engagement, and personal reflection among readers.

This book offers unique benefits to its readers. First, it presents one thousand unique statements that have not been said or written in the past. Hence, readers gain new knowledge by reading and reviewing these quotes. Second, additional descriptions of the forty quotes deepen readers' understanding about the statement that the author presents. Consequently, readers can also write their own quotes and descriptions based on their reading and understanding of the quotes and their description. Third, a real-life application of the quote is also demonstrated by presenting a story based on each quote. This story shows that the quote is not just a hypothetical statement but there is a real-life application of each quote, which further increases the effectiveness and significance of the quote.

People learn unique pieces of information from each quote and each statement has a real-life application; hence, people can learn the knowledge from each quote, and its application to real-life situations, which also increases the generalizability of each quote. As mentioned in the definition of quote, a quote also guides future work. Therefore, readers can further investigate each quote and conduct their research or discovery to further learn about the quote and its application. Fourth, an activity grounded in the quote is also presented, which engages diverse groups of audiences from various areas of life, such as family, school, community, and workplace. It fosters collaboration and engagement among these groups in the process of learning, which is informed by the quote. Fifth, critical thinking, engagement, and personal reflection is promoted by providing discussion questions about the quote. When people share their personal experiences, reflection, thinking, and expertise, it helps them to learn from one another, transform the knowledge, and promote a cocreation of new knowledge among readers. Hence, one quote shares many aspects of learning with a focus on a specific topic.

In sum, this book is not only to be used in academic settings, but it is also offered to those groups of audiences who are not related to any academic setting to grow and foster their learning on these quotes and promote discovery and exploration of these quotes among them through their application to real-life situations. Consequently, these quotes enhance readers' knowledge and understanding on the pieces of knowledge and information shared in each statement and also promote their critical thinking, personal engagement, and self-reflection.

Definition of a Quote

"Quotes are unique statements which are quite broad and general that people can relate and apply to their real-life situations and reflect on them to explore and guide future work."

ACCORDING TO THIS DEFINITION, quotes are a unique way to share and exchange knowledge and information. Quotes are comprised of unique statements of various kinds. These statements are quite broad such that they can be applied to several groups of the population who can relate these statements to themselves. People can apply quotes to their personal experiences and real-life situations and learn more about them. When people apply these quotes to themselves, these quotes provide them with appropriate solutions to their problems in a brief manner that readers can further understand and explore by accessing other sources of knowledge and information. For instance, if the quote shows that a parent-child attachment is important, particularly when the child is an infant or toddler, then after learning the statement, a primary caregiver (who is struggling to develop and maintain a healthy attachment and relationship with their child) can research other resources to understand the importance and benefits of parent-child statements and how they can be developed and fostered. Hence, quotes serve many purposes and facilitate readers in enhancing their relevant knowledge and application about the quote.

These quotes can also be treated as research questions that readers can investigate in different ways in the future based on their interest. A quote actively engages the audiences who can relate to it and keep using it for research and application purposes. For instance, if a quote states that love is a fundamental element in building healthy and sustainable relationships, readers can investigate this aspect of relationship by conducting a research study in the future if they are interested. Hence, a quote not only shares a brief piece of knowledge and information with readers, but it also provides readers with many opportunities to further delve into the depth of a statement and use different measures to investigate it.

QUOTE (A POEM)

Unique statements are called quotes
First I thought and then wrote
These statements are quite broad
Everyone can apply and promote
Unique ideas for people to note
Give future discovery, exploration, and hope
It puts together solutions to cope
People use it and have some control
It's one statement but a whole
This is the purpose of writing and the goal
Knowledge and information, this is its role
Spread all around when it rolls
Contains several advantages that I told
When people share, it floats
Concise, precise, and brief the most
People love it if this is the way you unfold
Whether you write in the office or home
Write a quote, in-person or remote
It reveals the hidden and showed
It's precious more than gold
There is nothing new or old
It always grows once you hold
When I write my quote
I feel I am in full control

Chapter 1: Dynamics of Friendship

This chapter shares that friends are a substantial asset for people. Best friends always stay together regardless of the situation. They support each other in tough times and celebrate good times with one another without showing any substantial differences in their moods, attitudes, and/or behaviors.

Quote

"Friends are those who share good and bad times with you without showing any difference"

Description of Quote

This quote shows the significance of friend relationships and how friends become useful for people in their lives. True friends are a great blessing for people. Friends may vary based on their sincerity, investments, and strength of relationship. For instance, some friends may be closer than others who show empathy, listen to one another, and help each other in tough times, whereas others may want to have some good time and leave in tough situations. Hence, it is important for people to understand the reality of friendship, learn about their friends, and choose those friends who are in their best interest.

What is your description of this quote? Write your description below:

_____

_____

_____

_____

_____
_____
_____
_____
_____
_____
_____

Story of Quote

CHARACTERS: *Jen, Jon, and Janel*

Jen, Jon, and Janel were good friends. They had unique personalities. They were delighted to spend good time with each other. They used to go for a walk daily, eat food together, and travel. Jen and Jon shared more about each other's likes and dislikes, whereas Janel was a bit reserved. Jen and Jon ignored it and kept spending exciting times with Janel. Everyone was supporting each other, enjoying themselves, and having fun. They also traveled to different places, took pictures of their pleasant memories, and had fun together.

One day, they were playing soccer and, unfortunately, Jen broke her leg. It was quite distressing and painful for her. At that moment, Jon and Janel called an ambulance and took Jen to the hospital. After the treatment, Jen's leg was saved because the injury was not quite severe. However, the doctor advised her to have bed rest for a few months. After a couple of days, Jen and Jon did not see Janel. She neither came to the hospital nor visited Jen's house. Jen and Jon were quite surprised at Janel's behaviors. They waited for her for a few weeks and then called her to inquire about the situation. Janel explained that she was not ready to show a commitment to that degree. She was having a joyful time but did not expect to support Jen and Jon in tough situations. After learning about Janel's intentions, Jen and Jon worked together, helped each other, and went through that tough situation. Jen recovered from her injury, and they again started to have a fun time with each other. Janel felt alone after some time, but it was too late for her.

Moral of the Story

Understand your friends

What is your story? Write your story below:

_____

_____

_____

_____

_____

_____

_____

_____

_____

_____

_____

Activity

Think about your friends and choose the one who is your best friend. Draw a portrait of your friend. Why is that individual your best friend? Share the qualities of your best friend.

Discussion Questions

1. Why are friends important in people's lives?

2. What are the qualities of good friends?

3. How do people choose their friends?

4. How do friends impact people's lives?

5. How do friends provide each other with support?

Chapter 2: The Greatness of Hearts

This chapter discusses that people experience the greatest potential of their heart when they love others and make concrete efforts to help and support them. The author demonstrates real-life situations of hardships, love, support, and compassion between people. He emphasizes the importance of loving and supporting others, which not only benefits others, but also becomes advantageous for those who help them.

Quote

"The greatness of hearts relates to loving others and showing compassion to them"

Description of Quote

The quote demonstrates the importance of loving others, showing empathy, and making concrete efforts to help and support others to resolve problems and address their needs. Since the nature of people's hearts is to love others, when people love others, they bring the potential of their hearts to a greater level.

What is your description of this quote? Write your description below:

_____
_____
_____
_____
_____
_____
_____

_____
_____
_____
_____

Story of Quote

CHARACTERS: *Brian, Jeremy, Lauren, and James*

Brian was a rich man who spent his whole life in working hard and, consequently, he became quite wealthy over time. However, he never thought about helping others financially, emotionally, or instrumentally. Even though financial support was more convenient for him due to his busy schedule, he never thought about helping others financially, which also limited his social connections and increased the degree of isolation for him. When he got older, he was feeling quite depressed, irritated, and bored because he did not have sufficient friends or social groups where he could spend his time. Though he was still quite active in his business, his heart was sad, and his mind was not quite efficient in terms of thinking about others.

One day, he heard about a family of three in his neighborhood who needed financial support. There was a couple, Jeremy (husband) and Lauren (wife), with his son (James). The family was living in poverty. Due to the winter season, they needed additional clothes. After learning about this family, Brian immediately met with them, asked politely and respectfully about their needs, and provided them with financial support. The family was so thankful to him for his generosity and support. After a few days, Brian started feeling substantial changes in himself. He was feeling very happy, his heart was very excited, his brain functioning was at its highest potential based on his age, and he wanted to do more with other families like this. The family who he helped and other families were coming to meet with Brian and he developed social connections and made sufficient friends, which also decreased his isolation and, consequently, his life became charming and exciting.

Moral of the Story

Love and help others

What is your story? Write your story below:

_____

_____

_____

_____

_____

_____

_____

_____

_____

_____

_____

_____

Activity

Look around in your neighborhood, meet with people, particularly those who have a low socioeconomic status or live in poverty. Ask them about their needs. How do they meet their basic needs? Which needs are left un-addressed? What can you do to help them?

Discussion Questions

1. What is poverty? What causes poverty?
2. How does poverty affect people's lives?
3. How does poverty impact children's well-being?
4. How can people work personally to address the issue of poverty?
5. How does personal financial support help people who live in poverty?

Chapter 3: Teamwork and Problem Solving

This chapter presents that people have the potential to resolve their problems themselves. They can generate their local resources to help themselves. In order to do that, people need to have empathy and compassion for one another to understand each other's problems and needs. Consequently, they can work together to address their problems and bring positive changes to their lives.

Quote

"When people have compassion for each other, many problems can be resolved at the microlevel of society"

Description of Quote

The quote reveals the importance and need for people to become compassionate for each other in the current society, work together, and resolve their local problems. All families have resources and strengths that they can utilize to grow and foster and simultaneously work together to identify their local needs and problems. It is important for people to show positive intentions, willingness to work together, and courage to address their problems and needs. Consequently, they need less external or macrolevel support to address their needs and issues because they become self-sufficient.

What is your description of this quote? Write your description below:

_____

_____

_____

_____

_____

_____

_____

_____

_____

_____

_____

Story of Quote

CHARACTERS: *David, Daniel, and Mary*

There were many families living in a local community. These families had sufficient wealth so, overall, the community was financially resourceful. However, the community was having problems with substance-use disorder. These families were thinking about their individual families but were not quite attentive to community situations and the different problems that were prevalent in their community. Once it happened that David's daughter Mary started having problems with substance-use disorder. Mary was going to college and spending her time in the neighborhood. Suddenly, her parents learned that she became addicted and started experiencing substance-use disorder. David (her father) and Daniel (her mother) were quite worried about this situation. They contacted a recovery center and relevant professionals in their neighborhood who helped Mary to deal with this problem. During her treatment, her parents also learned about the fact that this problem was quite prevalent in their neighborhood. All three members of the family worked in their local community, motivated people, and made them work together to resolve this problem. David's family shared their story and emphasized the need to think about others and their own families to prevent such problems. They further described that concrete efforts with good intentions were needed since the problem was quite severe in their neighborhood. All local families and individuals worked together and made their neighborhood free from substance-use disorder.

Moral of the Story

Work together to resolve local problems

What is your story? Write your story below:

_____
_____
_____
_____
_____
_____
_____
_____
_____
_____
_____
_____
_____

Activity

Take a tour of your community, meet with people, and visit the local offices of government and nongovernment organizations to learn which problems are prevalent in your community.

Discussion Questions

1. How do community problems affect adolescents and youth?
2. What problems are more serious than the others and why?
3. How can adolescents and youth be impacted by these problems?
4. What are the ways to resolve these problems?
5. How can community people work together to address these problems?

Chapter 4: Children Teach New Lessons to Parents

This chapter shares that not only parents teach and mentor their children, but sometimes children also teach their parents and provide them with substantial opportunities to learn how to raise their children and solve many problems. Children are the primary motivation for their parents. Although children bring demands and challenges to their parents, when parents see their children grown and successful, they get excited, motivated, and energized.

Quote

"Children teach parents new aspects and sensations of life"

Description of Quote

The quote describes that, although children are young and have less exposure to the outside world, because of their innocence, excitement, and creativity, they are also capable of demonstrating to and teaching their parents new things that their parents can learn from and be excited about.

What is your description of this quote? Write your description below:

_____
_____
_____
_____
_____
_____
_____

_____
_____
_____
_____

Story of Quote

CHARACTERS: *Patricia and Jennifer*

Patricia was a single working mother who had one child. Her name was Jennifer. The child was three years old. She was such an exciting and charming child who was always ready to explore, create, and engage in new and thrilling things. Due to these qualities, Patricia also got excited every time she observed her child doing new and creative things, which increased her positive feelings, pride, and satisfaction. By observing her daughter, Patricia started learning about children's developmental needs and changes because she wanted to know why and how her daughter was doing all these wonderful things. Consequently, she learned many new aspects of children that also helped her to reflect on her childhood experiences. She was also able to examine and compare her qualities with her daughter's qualities, which was so fascinating for her. She also learned how her child was developing and how she could further support her and foster her development. Consequently, her child became an important source of learning, joy, and satisfaction for her.

Moral of the Story

Young children are a source of learning for parents

What is your story? Write your story below:

_____
_____
_____
_____
_____
_____
_____
_____

Activity

If you have a young child, spend some time with them, observe them, write down what you observe, and then reflect on what you learn from these observations. If you don't have a child, you can also formally or informally observe a young child or children and notice new things that you learn from them.

Discussion Questions

1. What are the needs of young children?
2. How do parents learn young children's needs?
3. How do parents know what their children feel?
4. How do young children teach their parents new things about life?
5. How do children become a source of sensation, joy, and satisfaction for their parents?

Chapter 5: Understanding Each Other's Needs

This chapter presents the importance of those people who understand others' feelings. For instance, best friends see each other's face and they immediately understand the mood and feelings of one another. If one friend needs something, the other friend immediately figures it out even though the one does not share it. These people are quite special in life; hence, people who have such people in their life need to recognize their importance and work together to keep them in their life.

Quote

"When they see your face and understand your feelings and needs, they are quite special for you"

Description of Quote

The quote shows the importance of sensitive and caring partners in a healthy relationship who carefully observe each other, understand feelings, and address each other's needs. People are usually considered so fortunate who have such a partner in their intimate relationship. More importantly, when people have a wonderful and caring partner, it is important not to take them for granted because they are a quite special partner.

What is your description of this quote? Write your description below:

_____
_____
_____
_____

_____

_____

_____

_____

_____

_____

_____

Story of Quote

CHARACTERS: *Barbara, Richard, and John*

Barbara was in a toxic relationship and her partner Richard was quite abusive and controlling. That relationship was negatively impacting her well-being, productivity, and social relations. Consequently, she broke up and left her partner, Richard. It took her quite a while to come out of that trauma. She was able to find John, who was a decent individual. At the beginning of their relationship, Barbara was a bit quiet, she didn't want to talk a lot because she wanted to learn more about John, and she was not sure about the certainty of their relationship. John was observing Barbara and reading the situation. He was understanding Barbara's feelings, and he realized that he needed to build trust to make her feel comfortable. He was also trying to understand her trauma and he realized that he could help her in this situation to stay normal in her current relationship. Consequently, he was making additional efforts and investing his time, such as washing dishes, scheduling dates, buying tickets for movies, etc. Consequently, Barbara built her trust in John. She started sharing about herself and the previous relationship. John was quite positive and responsive in these conversations. He listened quite attentively, and both partners became expressive and reflective in their conversations. Barbara started to feel more comfortable in her conversations with John. Over time, she forgot her trauma and stayed normal in her current relationship. Both partners worked together to foster and sustain their healthy and happy relationship.

Moral of the Story

Don't take special partners for granted

What is your story? Write your story below:

_____
_____
_____
_____
_____
_____
_____
_____
_____
_____
_____
_____

Activity

Talk to your partner to learn about their feelings and relationship needs. Examine yourself to assess the degree to which you understand their feelings and address their needs. Repeat it for yourself.

Discussion Questions

1. How do partners express their feelings?
2. What are the relationship needs?
3. What should they do to address each other's relationship needs?
4. How should partners learn each other's feelings and needs?
5. Why are learning and addressing partners' feelings and needs important?

Chapter 6: When You Can't Compare Their Smile

This chapter presents the idea that the person who people love is the most valuable for them. Their company and smile are priceless for them. People get excited due to their company. Such a person gives hope, happiness, and motivation for life. No smile looks like them and no one can be compared with them. When this is the case, people are in love with them.

Quote

"When you can't compare any smile to the one who makes you excited, you are in love with them"

Description of Quote

The quote uncovers the importance of that person who is loved by someone. The individual who falls in love with them loves their smile, which they cannot compare with any other person's smile because no smile can excite them to that degree.

What is your description of this quote? Write your description below:

_____
_____
_____
_____
_____
_____
_____
_____
_____

_____
_____
_____

Story of Quote

CHARACTERS: *Joseph and Jessica*

Joeseph fell in love with Jessica. He wanted to spend all his time with her. He kept thinking about her. He was not quite wealthy, and he used to do a nonstandard job. Due to the nature of his job, he used to get tired and exhausted but when he met with Jessica every day after his work and she admired Joesph's hard work and dedication with her pleasant smile and welcoming face, Joesph felt excited, all his worries, tiredness, and exhaustion disappeared. Though the time he spent with Jessica was quite short, he used to feel that he was in a different world where joy, excitement, and happiness spread all around and there were no signs of worries. He used to think about other faces, smiles, and interactions that he had throughout the day but he couldn't compare anyone with Jessica's face and her smile. He discovered that he fell in love with her and that's why he only saw her as the most important person of his life who inspired and motivated him to work hard, be punctual, and disciplined throughout the day, because he had to get the reward of her delightful smile and bright face. Jessica also fell in love with Joseph to the same degree and both partners couldn't imagine living without each other.

Moral of the Story

Love and loved ones are special

What is your story? Write your story below:

_____
_____
_____
_____
_____
_____
_____

_____
_____
_____

Activity

If you fell in love with someone, think about them, their smile and face, and how they excite you and give a motivation to your life. Think about the degree of their importance in your life. If you never fell in love with someone, then find a person who has and ask these questions of them.

Discussion Questions

1. What is love?

2. How do people know they love someone?

3. How do people express love and its feelings?

4. How does a person whom you love become so important in your life?

5. Why do they excite you?

Chapter 7: Friendship Without Formalities

This chapter shares the qualities of friendship as it builds on trust, support, and enjoyment. People spend time with their friends and share their private information without feeling any formalities and limitations. Friends are each other's source of relaxation and entertainment.

Quote

"Friendship is holding hands, trusting each other, and living together without any formalities"

Description of Quote

The quote demonstrates the significance of friendship. It is a relationship which doesn't require any formalities, people become spontaneous and honest in expressing their feelings because they feel their friends are a safe environment and people. Consequently, friends support each other, build trust, and happily live together.

What is your description of this quote? Write your description below:

_____
_____
_____
_____
_____
_____
_____
_____
_____
_____

Story of Quote

CHARACTERS: *Karen, Lisa, Charles, and Thomas*

Karen, Lisa, and Charles were best friends. They built their relationship steadily over time. They invested a lot of time, energy, and effort to build trust and a sense of connection between them. They now enjoy the company of each other. They hold hands, visit new places regularly, participate in outdoor activities, and spend enjoyable time with each other. They are each other's support and resource. Lisa's father Thomas was struggling to manage his family expenses. He was a single father so he didn't have a partner who could share the household's bills and expenses with him. Due to such a tough situation, Lisa and Thomas were not having a peaceful and joyful time in the family and it affected the family's functioning. Lisa discussed her family situation with Karen and Charles because she trusted them. Karen knew a nongovernment organization who provided financial support and counseling to low-socioeconomic single-parent families. Charles offered his vehicle to visit the organization's office. They first went to Lisa's house, shared this information with Thomas, and convinced him that it could be a wonderful opportunity for their family. When Thomas agreed, they called the nongovernment organization and scheduled a meeting. After a few days, when they met with the staff of the organization, they not only provided immediate financial support to Thomas but also offered professional services to him for starting a small-scale business. This was wonderful support from the nongovernment organization for Thomas and his family. Thomas liked the small-scale business idea and decided to work with them in the future. Thomas and Lisa worked hard to establish their small business, and Lisa's friends supported them in their small business. Consequently, they made wonderful progress in their small business and started living a happy life.

Moral of the Story

Friends are valuable support and supporters

What is your story? Write your story below:

_____

_____

_____

_____

_____

_____

_____

_____

_____

_____

_____

_____

Activity

Think about your few best friends. Why are they important in your life? What type of support do you provide to each other? Why is having friends so important for people?

Discussion Questions

1. What is friendship?
2. Why is friendship important for people?
3. What type of support do friends provide to each other?
4. Why is trust important in friend relationships?
5. Discuss the joys of friendship.

Chapter 8: Wish to Travel with Them for Your Whole Life

This chapter presents a love relationship between people. When people fall in love with a person, they want to spend each moment of their life with them. They want to listen to them all the time and not get tired, instead they get excited. They want to travel with that person, eat, and sleep. They only see that person who they love in the entire world.

Quote

"When you wish to travel with them for your entire life and know that you will not get tired, rather become excited, you are in love with them"

Description of Quote

The quote demonstrates the significance and power of love. When people want to spend all their time with their loved one, including pleasant and tough times, they love each other. They get excited with the pleasant time and don't get tired with the tough time because they want to stay and travel with one another for their entire life.

What is your description of this quote? Write your description below:

_____
_____
_____
_____
_____
_____
_____
_____

_____
_____
_____
_____

Story of Quote

CHARACTERS: *Mathew and Ashley*

Mathew and Ashley were high school sweethearts. They liked each other but never expressed their love for each other. When school finished, both left the town, but they had love for each other in their hearts. Once they met in a tourist place where they both came to visit. They were quite surprised to see each other. They still had so much love and positive feelings for each other. At this time, they were quite matured to express their love and emotions for each other. They spent most of their time together. One night, it was chilly, the moon was shing on the sky, stars were all around the moon, they were listening to live music and whispering with each other. Mathew started their high school stories, Ashley got excited, Mathew took it as an opportunity and invited Ashley to share more stories. Then Mathew told her how much he loved her during their high school time. He expressed his feelings and described the difficulty that he experienced sharing his feelings with Ashley before. Ashley was very surprised because she had quite the same feelings for Mathew. They then realized that they loved each other. They hugged and kissed each other and promised to stay with each other for their entire life. They also planned to visit the entire world together. This moment was so exciting and fun for them.

Moral of the Story

Love shows anytime

What is your story? Write your story below:

_____
_____
_____
_____
_____

_____

_____

_____

_____

_____

Activity

Meet with high school sweethearts and learn about their feelings. Share the above story of Mathew and Ashley with them. Learn about their views and opinions about the story. Talk to them and discover their stories and plans for the future.

Discussion Questions

1. Why is love important in a relationship?
2. What are the feelings of love that people experience?
3. What are the emotions which are accompanied by love?
4. When should people express their love?
5. What are good times and ways to share feelings of love?

Chapter 9: Various Forms of Love

This chapter discusses the form, degree, and nature of love as it exists in all types of relationship. For instance, love exists in a parent-child relationship, it also exists in a couple relationship, and it is prevalent in a friend relationship. However, its form, degree, and nature are changed based on the type of relationship that exists. It is important that people acknowledge that all relationships are grounded in love, and they need to act on it to maintain the same or greater degree of love in their relationship.

Quote

"Love exists in all types of relationships with its different forms, degrees, and nature; people need to feel and act on it"

Description of Quote

The quote highlights the importance of love and how it is prevalent in all types of relationships with different degrees and nature. Without love and positive feelings, relationships cannot be successful. People's feelings, experiences, and expectations may vary based on the type of relationship. All types of relationships which are grounded in love provide people with joy and happiness.

What is your description of this quote? Write your description below:

_____

_____

_____

_____

_____

_____

_____

_____

_____

_____

_____

Story of Quote

CHARACTERS: *Mark, Emily, Donald, and Kim*

Mark and Emily got married after facing a divorce and successfully coming out of that phase. They both had a child from the previous relationship. Mark had his son, Donald, and Emily had her daughter, Kim, from their previous relationship and, subsequently, they created a stepfamily. Mark and Emily were quite sensible and mature and knew the challenges and opportunities that existed between their family members. At the beginning, their children didn't develop a good relationship because of different reasons, which affected all relationships in the family. Then Mark and Emily discussed and analyzed the situation and decided to have several meetings with their children. Both explained and demonstrated that they loved both children and they also loved each other as a couple: "Based on the type of relationship, the form, degree, and nature of love may change. For instance, we as partners love each other and become intimate whereas we love you as our children and our love is different for you. However, love accompanies positive feelings and emotions. Please remember that we love you both; as stepsiblings also develop your love and positive relationship. It is possible that you may not develop love and positive feelings toward each other right away, but it will happen over time with concrete effort and sincere intentions." After these informal meetings with their children, the relationships between them all substantially improved.

Moral of the Story

Love may vary with relationships

What is your story? Write your story below:

_____

_____

_____
_____
_____
_____
_____
_____
_____
_____
_____
_____

Activity

Meet with a stepfamily and read this story for them. Learn about their relationship dynamics. Discover if any of the situations described in the above story apply to them. Explore appropriate solutions to the situation they share with you.

Discussion Questions

1. What are the different forms of relationships?

2. Why do the degree and nature of love differ based on the relationship type?

3. How should people act to address relationship issues and needs?

4. How do people discover that love exists in their relationship?

5. How do people create love and positive feelings in their relationships?

Chapter 10: Strengths of Flowers

This chapter highlights the significance of flowers. Flowers are a symbol of love. They are used to grow love, strengthen relationships, and promote forgiveness. Hence, people need to use the strengths of flowers to initiate and build positive relationships, remove conflicts and promote forgiveness, and grow love in their relationships.

Quote

"Flowers have hidden strengths which promote love, relationships, and forgiveness between people"

Description of Quote

The quote shows the power and strengths of flowers in building love and relationships and promoting forgiveness between people. Flowers have hidden strengths that change the mood of people, decrease resentment, and bring people together. Flowers signify happiness, togetherness, and joy. Hence, the use of flowers is important when people aim at building relationships with others.

What is your description of this quote? Write your description below:

_____
_____
_____
_____
_____
_____
_____

_____

_____
_____
_____

Story of Quote

CHARACTERS: *Paul and Amanda*

Paul and Amanda were best friends. Other than Amanda, Paul didn't have any friends. He shared his situation with Amanda: he tried to make many friends but due to certain reasons that he was not even sure about, he couldn't sustain those relationships. Amanda discovered from Paul the reasons why he wasn't maintaining his relationships with others. These were the primary reasons that came up after Amanda's discussion with Paul. The first reason was, though Paul was initiating a friend relationship, he was not preserving it through effective communication, connection, or small gifts. The second reason was Paul's low temperament: he used to get angry, which created resentment between him and his friends. Amanda told him the strengths and power of flowers and what they signify. She explained that he should visit his friends, give them flowers, and show his appreciation and respect for them and their relationship with him. She also explained that flowers can reduce resentment and anger between him and his friends so he should use that power and strength in promoting love, positive relationships, and forgiveness, which is why people use flowers for happy events such as weddings, birthdays, engagements, etc. After taking Amanda's advice, Paul visited each of his friends who he was disconnected from, gave them flowers, and spent some valuable time with positive feelings and discussion about flowers and what they signify. A few weeks later, when Amanda met with Paul and asked about his actions and the situation with his friends, Paul was pleased to share that he regained all his friends who had left him, and he was so happy to have them again. Amanda was so excited to hear that, and they both also had a wonderful time that night.

Moral of the Story

Flowers strenghten relationships with people

What is your story? Write your story below:

_____
_____
_____
_____
_____
_____
_____
_____
_____
_____
_____
_____

Activity

Take some beautiful flowers and meet with your friend who has not been in touch with you for a while. Share the above story and ask their views about and experiences with flowers. Have positive conversations with them and regain the connection with that friend which you lost earlier.

Discussion Questions

1. What do flowers signify?
2. What is the importance of flowers?
3. Discuss the strengths of flowers.
4. How do flowers promote love, relationships, and forgiveness?
5. How do you use flowers to strengthen your relationship?

Chapter 11: When They Are Not with You

This chapter presents the importance of loved ones in people's lives. People become very happy and excited when they are with their loved ones regardless of the type of outside weather or environment. When they are not with their loved ones, even the spring season does not give them such charm and excitement as it is supposed to do.

Quote

"All seasons of love become irrelevant when they are not with you"

Description of Quote

The quote shows the importance of togetherness for people who love each other. Lovers want to spend all their time with one another. They need to make concerted efforts to grow and sustain their relationship because their relationship is quite sensitive since they love each other and become emotionally connected with each other. However, when, due to any reason, lovers separate from each other, life becomes boring, they lose motivation and excitement. Even those seasons which they feel unique and exciting for themselves do not give the same energy without their partner.

What is your description of this quote? Write your description below:

_____

_____

_____

_____

_____

_____

_____
_____
_____
_____
_____

Story of Quote

CHARACTERS: *Kevin and Melissa*

Kevin and Melissa fell in love at first sight with each other. They were very emotionally attached to each other. They took care of each other and their relationship at the beginning. As time passed, they got busy in their work and family matters. Consequently, they neglected the sensitivity and importance of their relationship. They were not spending adequate time with one another, there was less sharing between them, and they were not making sufficient plans to foster and maintain their relationship. After some time, they did not prevent disagreements, resentment, and conflicts from their relationship. As a result, they faced a breakup. It was quite difficult for them to survive without each other after their breakup. They got depressed, their motivation and excitement for life substantially reduced, and their productivity went down as well. Although they still had love for each other, they just did not realize the sensitivity of their love relationship, and were lacking the appropriate effort they needed to make to grow and sustain their relationship. One day, Melissa called Kevin, who was thinking about her, and explained her situation. They decided to meet at a restaurant. Both reflected on their relationship, which helped them to uncover the mistakes they made that ruined their relationship. They found out they did not understand the sensitivity of their relationship, which also limited their efforts to grow and maintain it. They apologized to each other and promised to work together to grow and foster their relationship. After some time, they both felt a substantial and positive change in their relationship that also positively affected their health and well-being.

Moral of the Story

Understand the sensitivity of your love relationship

What is your story? Write your story below:

_____
_____
_____
_____
_____
_____
_____
_____
_____
_____
_____
_____

Activity

Meet with a couple who faced a breakup and read the above story, either before both partners or with one partner at a time, whichever is convenient for you. Ask about the problems they had in their relationship that caused their breakup and learn about their future plans in that regard. Ask whether they could apply the above story and find a solution to their relationship problem.

Discussion Questions

1. What are breakups?
2. Why do breakups happen?
3. What are the reasons for breakups?
4. How do partners resolve their conflicts?
5. What are some suggestions to prevent breakups?

Chapter 12: Eyes Send Messages and Hearts Receive

This chapter shares the chemistry between lovers. Lovers are connected by their hearts to one another, they understand the feelings and experiences of each other without having those explained to them. They read each other's eyes and learn what the other person feels. Lovers send messages through their eyes and their hearts receive those messages because lovers' hearts are connected due falling in love with one another.

Quote

"Eyes send messages and hearts receive them between people who are in love"

Description of Quote

The quote highlights the significance of hearts and eyes that function substantially in love. People's hearts are connected to those whom they love. When their hearts are attached to each other in terms of feelings, they feel and receive each other's messages in their hearts. People's eyes also play an important role because lovers show the heart's feelings from their eyes and when it is a true love both partners send message from their eyes and since their hearts are connected, they feel and receive those messages. Hence, love is a unique experience for them.

What is your description of this quote? Write your description below:

_____

_____

_____
_____
_____
_____
_____
_____
_____
_____
_____
_____

Story of Quote

CHARACTERS: *Joshua and Carol*

Joshua and Carol were in love with each other. Their relationship was an ideal relationship. Their hearts were connected to each other such that they could look at each other's face and body language and feel in their heart what the other partner was feeling and thinking about. It was such a true love. Their eyes were also quite functional in sending messages. They became masters of reading each other's eyes. One day, Carol was so depressed after work, but she did not want to bother Joshua. Joshua immediately looked into her eyes and felt in his heart that she was very depressed. After asking about it a few times, Carol admitted that she was very depressed and, due to the situation, her mood was also not good. They went on a date. Carol discussed her problem and the reasons for her bad mood, both partners explored constructive solutions, and, consequently, resolved Carol's problem. Joushua and Carol were having a unique experience in their love relationship. They knew how important this relationship was for them; hence, they were giving it appropriate time, making concrete efforts, and supporting each other to grow and foster it.

Moral of the Story

Be supportive of your partner

What is your story? Write your story below:

_____
_____
_____

_____

_____

_____

_____

_____

_____

_____

_____

Activity

Meet with a couple who are in love with each other. Read the above story for them. Ask them to share their relationship dynamics in the context of the story. Invite them to share their experiences and identify the similarities and differences between what they explained and what was written in the story.

Discussion Questions

1. Why are relationships important?

2. How do relationships become people's strengths?

3. How should people maintain their relationships?

4. How do partners resolve problems in constructive ways?

5. How do positive relationships increase the health and well-being of a couple?

Chapter 13: Feelings, Hearts, and People Are Connected

This chapter describes the dynamics of love between people. People love each other based on positive feelings for the other person. Due to such feelings, people's hearts start liking the other person. Consequently, they want to connect with that person who they have feelings for because they love them.

Quote

"Feelings connect hearts and hearts connect people"

Description of Quote

The quote demonstrates the connections between feelings, hearts, and people, particularly when people fall in love with one another. When people love each other, they feel something different for each other and such feelings are created in their hearts. When they have such feelings in their hearts, they want to meet with each other, talk and spend time together, and learn about each other. Hence, their hearts' feelings motivate them to connect with each other.

What is your description of this quote? Write your description below:

_____
_____
_____
_____
_____
_____

_____

_____

_____

_____

_____

Story of Quote

CHARACTERS: *Rachel and Patrick*

Rachel was working in a coffee shop. This was her part-time job, and she was a full-time student in a university. She was so nice to her customers, who praised her work and her dealing with them. Patrick also used to come every day several times for a coffee in her shop. They talked a lot while buying and selling a cup of coffee. They both were having a wonderful time with each other. Both suddenly realized that they were having different and special feelings for one another. Initially, both ignored this, but when they acknowledged these feelings, they experienced the motivation to meet and greater affection for each other. They both wanted to spend more time together, were eager to learn about each other, and stay with one another most of the time. Their hearts were bringing them together due to such special feelings they had for one another. One day, Patrick asked Rachel to go for dinner with him. Rachel agreed without any hesitation. They had a wonderful time with each other. After having dinner, Patrick started explaining his feelings for Rachel, who acknowledged and appreciated his love. Rachel also expressed her feelings for Patrick, which made him very happy and excited. They both were excited and delighted to have each other. Consequently, they formally started dating and developing a more intimate relationship.

Moral of the Story

Love, feelings, and hearts connect people

What is your story? Write your story below:

_____

_____

_____

_____

Activity

Reach out to a couple who are in love with one another and share the above story with them. Ask about their story, feelings, and experiences of the relationship.

Discussion Questions

1. What are feelings?
2. Why are feelings important between people?
3. What are the linkages between feelings and heart?
4. How do feelings of hearts bring people together?
5. What are the experiences of people who are in love?

Chapter 14: Secrets of Building Love Relationships

This chapter shares important factors that are essential for building healthy love relationships, such as trust, respect, and sacrifice. In a healthy relationship, both people trust one another; consequently, they feel comfortable sharing their private information with each other. Both partners respect each other and show empathy and compassion for one another. Hence, trust, respect, and sacrifice are essential elements of a love relationship.

Quote

"Trust, respect, and sacrifice are essential elements for building love relationships"

Description of Quote

The quote shows the importance of different elements, such as trust, respect, and sacrifice, in building love relationships. Love is exciting but simultaneously it is quite difficult for people to maintain the same degree of love in their relationship. Consequently, they make concrete efforts to grow and maintain their love relationship.

What is your description of this quote? Write your description below:

_____
_____
_____
_____
_____
_____

Story of Quote

CHARACTERS: *Maria and Frank*

Maria and Frank were in a relationship. They both fell in love at first sight with one another. They understood that their relationship was exciting at the beginning but in order to successfully sustain it, they needed to build trust, show respect and appreciation for one another, and demonstrate sacrifice and compassion for each other. They started sharing about their own self, past, and future with one another. Though they had not received any formal training or education on building an intimate relationship, they were quite mindful in terms of the degree of sharing their personal information with each other over time. They were sharing their personal information with one another but not making each other overwhelmed with the amount of information. Consequently, they were building trust because they both were positively listening and responding to one another. They were supporting each other in their plans for the future. They were also respecting each other verbally and nonverbally and demonstrating appreciation for one another and the relationship they had formed. They also provided one another with constructive feedback to resolve any problems. They were working together like a team to initiate and pursue their goals and dreams. Although they were having some financial problems because Frank lost his job, and due to the economic situation in the country, they worked hard together to build trust with each other in their relationship, create a respectful and appreciative environment, and show support, sacrifice, and compassion for one another. They successfully dealt with these tough situations and sustained a healthy intimate relationship.

Moral of the Story

Trust building and appreciation are essential for sustainable relationships

What is your story? Write your story below:

_____
_____
_____
_____
_____
_____
_____
_____
_____
_____
_____
_____

Activity

Reach out to a couple and share the above story. Discover whether they resonate with any parts of the story and their real-life situation. Ask about how they use essential elements, such as trust, respect, and sacrifice, in building their relationship.

Discussion Questions

1. What are trust, respect, and appreciation?
2. What is the role of trust in building a love relationship?
3. How do partners show compassion for one another?
4. How does trust help couples in dealing with tough situations?
5. What are the qualities of a healthy intimate relationship?

Chapter 15: Linkages Between Poetry and Writing

This chapter highlights the linkages between poetry and writing. Poetry relates to writing because writers express their sentiments, feelings, and thoughts when they write poetry. Poetry helps readers to imagine, relate, and get excited. Hence, poetry is a pleasant form of writing, which makes people happy and excited.

Quote

"Poetry reflects the beauty of writing"

Description of Quote

The quote highlights the effectiveness and role of writing in poetry. Poetry is a pleasant and important form of writing. When people cannot express their love and feelings to another person, they use poetry to convey their feelings and emotions to that person. Sometimes, people do not understand their feelings and emotions when they experience love, but poetry helps them to understand and explain these feelings in a positive and comprehensive manner.

What is your description of this quote? Write your description below:

_____

_____

_____

_____

_____

_____

Story of Quote

CHARACTERS: *Olivia and Tyler*

Olivia and Tyler were studying in a high school. Both were seniors and quite good in their studies. Tyler started liking Olivia, but he was a bit shy. Suddenly, his liking converted into love. First, he could not understand his feelings for Olivia. Then he started reading poetry books and learned how people felt and expressed their love when they had special feelings for the other person. Over time, he started expressing his feelings in writing. He was writing how much he loved Olivia and that he wanted to spend his time with her and share his personal life with her. He also wrote that she was a very special person in his life who motivated him, disciplined his life, and increased his productivity in various areas of his life. He wrote several pages of poetry in which he expressed his love and feelings for Olivia. On Olivia's birthday, he gave this mini book along with flowers to her. Olivia initially did not understand about his book but when she thoroughly studied it, examined Tyler's behaviors that he had been showing to her for the past year, and recognized the hints in the book that he provided to relate his poetry with Olivia, she was very impressed, the poetry also created special feelings in her heart for Tyler. Next day, she met Tyler and thanked him for his gift. She also expressed her feelings for Tyler. They both got very happy and excited about the situation. Tyler was especially proud of himself for the path he adopted to attract Olivia and express his feelings to her. They both successfully formed a healthy love relationship.

Moral of the Story

Poetry speaks and conveys messages

What is your story? Write your story below:

_____

_____

_____

_____

_____

_____

_____

_____

_____

Activity

Visit your local library, check out a few poetry books, read those books which are particularly written on love and romantic relationships, write notes, compare it with the above story, and share it with your friends.

Discussion Questions

1. What is poetry?
2. How does writing grow poetry and people's expressions?
3. What is the role of poetry in love relationships?
4. How do people use poetry to express their feelings?
5. How do poetry and writing connect people?

Chapter 16: The Role of Constructive Listening and Speaking

This chapter demonstrates the significance of constructive listening and speaking in improving people's knowledge. When people use their time in different settings with various people by carefully listening to them and clearly conveying their message, they utilize their time effectively, build positive relationships with one another, and improve their personal knowledge. Hence, constructive listening and speaking are essential qualities of people to improve their personal knowledge and develop positive interpersonal relationships.

Quote

"Constructive listening and speaking increase people's knowledge and build positive interpersonal relationships"

Description of Quote

The quote shows the importance and role of constructive listening and speaking in fostering people's knowledge, especially those who are doing it deliberately in their relationships whether it is a personal, friend, or professional relationship.

What is your description of this quote? Write your description below:

_____

_____

_____

_____

_____

_____

_____

_____

_____

_____

_____

Story of Quote

CHARACTERS: *Heather and Jack*

Heather and Jack were best friends. They were also studying together in high school. They would spend most of their time together. They were quite thoughtful about the importance of their time. Hence, they were using constructive speaking and listening to build their knowledge. Each day, one person (one day for Heather and the other day for Jack) prepared a topic on a matter their local communities were experiencing, such as homelessness, education, health, substance use, mass violence, etc. The person who was responsible for preparing the topic explained it to the other. That person would also write and share some notes they had prepared for the topic with the other. They were carefully listening, asking questions, and providing constructive feedback. Both friends were carrying out a healthy and constructive discussion and exploring appropriate solutions for those problems. Such constructive speaking and listening practices substantially increased their personal, interpersonal, and professional knowledge and skills.

Moral of the Story

Constructive speaking and listening have substantial significance for people

What is your story? Write your story below:

_____

_____

_____

_____

_____

_____

_____

_____

_____

_____

Activity

Meet with a group of friends, share the above story, ask them how they spend their time together. Ask them to allocate a day to practice constructive speaking and listening as described in the above story. Follow up with them and learn the significance of constructive speaking and listening that they practiced.

Discussion Questions

1. What are constructive speaking and listening?

2. Why are constructive speaking and listening important?

3. How do they build people's knowledge?

4. How should people use constructive speaking and listening in their relationships?

5. Describe the benefits of constructive speaking and listening.

Chapter 17: The Heart and Eyes in Love

This chapter presents the dynamics of love as it starts with the feelings of heart that people create for another person. Love is an emotional aspect of people's lives. Hence, when people fall in love with another person, their heart becomes full of emotion and positive feelings about the other person. These feelings and emotions stay and reflect in their eyes.

Quote

"The ocean of love starts from the heart and stays in the eyes"

Description of Quote

The quote describes that when people fall in love with one another, they receive positive energy and feelings in their heart about each other. The heart is the center of love where feelings of love for others generate and start, and these feelings show through people's eyes. Hence, the heart and eyes are essential elements in a love relationship.

What is your description of this quote? Write your description below:

_____
_____
_____
_____
_____
_____
_____
_____

_____
_____
_____

Story of Quote

CHARACTERS: *Justin and Anna*

Justin and Anna were pursuing their undergraduate degree. They were spending substantial time together and helping each other in their studies. They were very good friends and supporters of one another. Both started feeling something else for each other over time. Their hearts got excited when they were meeting with one another, they were not staying away from each other, they wanted to spend all their time together. Their hearts were feeling differently, and their emotions and excitement were at their peak. Initially they were hiding the feelings they had for one another but since they knew each other quite well, they could have looked into each other's eyes and noticed their feelings for one another. One day, Anna made up a story and read it to Justin. She explained in her story what she was feeling for Justin but did not explicitly mention that this was actually their own story. Justin felt that the story also resonated with his feelings. He expressed that he was feeling that the story described his own situation. Anna smiled and said that this was her situation as well that she wanted to share. Both smiled, hugged, and kissed, and they started a new relationship with love, intimacy, and affection.

Moral of the Story

Love does not hide

What is your story? Write your story below:

_____
_____
_____
_____
_____
_____
_____
_____

_____
_____
_____
_____

Activity

Meet with a college couple who love each other, share the above story, ask about their story, compare both stories, learn about their relationship, excitement, and the challenges associated with their relationship.

Discussion Questions

1. What do people feel about love in their heart?
2. How does the heart connect with the eyes?
3. How do eyes show what the heart feels?
4. Why can lovers not hide their love and feelings from each other?
5. What is a healthy love relationship?

Chapter 18: Parents' Challenges and Rewards

This chapter describes the situation of contemporary parenting. Although parenting is extremely difficult today, it is simultaneously quite rewarding for parents because they get hope, energy, and pride when they raise their children and see them growing. Their child's smile helps them recover from adversity and helps them forget the challenges associated with the demands of their child.

Quote

"Parenting is one of the most challenging but rewarding roles in society, and one smile of a child changes how parents feel"

Description of Quote

The quote demonstrates the importance of parenting in contemporary society. Although parenting is quite challenging, it also comes with pride and rewards when parents successfully raise their children and their children appreciate them by smiling, hugging, and kissing them.

What is your description of this quote? Write your description below:

_____
_____
_____
_____
_____
_____
_____

Story of Quote

CHARACTERS: *Amy, Gary, and Emma*

Amy and Gary were new parents. Although they planned their first child, they neither received any formal education nor attended any program on parenting. Hence, it was quite challenging for them to raise their child, Emma, at the beginning when she was born. They both were working parents; hence, it was difficult for them at the beginning to manage childcare responsibilities. They managed their work schedule by doing alternate shifts. Emma was showing irritating behavior, she was crying during the night and had difficulties taking her food. Both parents faced substantial challenges at the beginning but did not lose heart. Although they were tired, exhausted, and stressed due to their work, family, and the newborn's responsibilities, when Emma was smiling, her parents holding her, kissing her, and hugging her, all their tension, exhaustion, and stress had disappeared. They were very satisfied and happy as parents and were quite proud of performing this role. When Emma was six years old, things became normal, both parents worked together, and enjoyed their relaxing time.

Moral of the Story

Parenting is challenging but rewarding

What is your story? Write your story below:

Activity

Meet with a couple who are recent parents, share the above story with them, and ask about their challenges and rewards in raising their child. Learn about their experiences of parenting and discover what they feel about their role as parents, ask about the importance of the child in their life.

Discussion Questions

1. What is parenting?
2. What challenges do parents in current society face?
3. What are the rewards for parents of parenting?
4. What is the importance of a child in the parents' life?
5. How do parents feel about their role as parents? What support do they need?

Chapter 19: Siblings Are Important Mentors

This chapter explains the role of siblings in each other's life. Siblings learn from and teach each other every day. When siblings learn from each other, such education and skills are quite impactful because they understand each other well. So, siblings' mentoring and education is very effective for one another. Hence, parents need to create a culture where siblings create learning and support for one another.

Quote

"Siblings are mentors who guide and educate each other every day, and parents need to promote such practices"

Description of Quote

The quote highlights the importance of positive siblings' relationships. Siblings learn from and educate each other about new things daily. Since they have a quite close relationship, they are more likely to learn from each other effectively. Hence, parents need to build positive relationships between their children and promote such mentoring practices between them.

What is your description of this quote? Write your description below:

_____

_____

_____

_____

_____

_____

_____
_____
_____
_____
_____

Story of Quote

CHARACTERS: Jason, Laura, Sharon, and Edward

Jeson and Laura had a happy family of four including themselves. They had two children, Sharon and Edward. Both parents worked hard to build healthy and positive relationships between their children. They avoided any favoritism and practiced positive and fair parenting with them, which not only made a positive impact on the parent-child relationship, but also built a healthy sibling relationship in their family. Both siblings behaved quite well with each other. They played together, exercised, ate, and pursued interesting hobbies. Edward was good at computer use, whereas Sharon was quite an expert in writing. Edward mentored Sharon on how to use computers. He gave her an important lesson every day. After some time, Sharon became an expert like Edward. She also discovered that she could write on the computer. So, she offered Edward a writing lesson on the computer. Edward needed additional assistance in his writing. Over time Edward also became an expert in writing like Sharon. Due to teamwork, both siblings learned important skills from each other. When they told their parents about their mentoring practices and new skills, Jason and Laura were very delighted. They praised their children and were very proud of them.

Moral of the Story

Siblings are each other's mentors

What is your story? Write your story below:

_____
_____
_____
_____
_____
_____

Activity

Meet with siblings in a family, share the above story with them, and learn about their mentoring practices. Discover how their parents build their positive relationships, and how siblings learn from and educate each other.

Discussion Questions

1. What is a sibling relationship?
2. Why are siblings' relationships important?
3. How do siblings learn from each other?
4. What are positive parenting practices?
5. How do parents promote mentoring practices between their children?

Chapter 20: Parents' Positive Relationships and Children's Development

This chapter presents the role of parents in their children's lives. When parents show compassion for their children and make concrete efforts to build positive relationship with their children, their children show positive developmental outcomes, such as self-confidence, high academic performance, social and emotional regulation, and self-esteem. Hence, parents need to understand their children and build healthy relationships with them to facilitate their growth and positive development in contemporary society.

Quote

"Parents' positive relationships with their children and youth are one of the determinants of their development in contemporary societies"

Description of Quote

The quote highlights the importance of parents' positive and healthy relationships with their children and youth. Given the high demands of work and family, parents have limited time to spend with their children and youth. On the other hand, due to diverse and complex contemporary societies, advancement of media and technology, neighborhood characteristics, and school expectations, children need to connect with their parents and build positive and healthy relationships with them, which ensures their growth and development.

What is your description of this quote? Write your description below:

_____

_____

_____

_____

_____

_____

_____

_____

_____

_____

_____

Story of Quote

CHARACTERS: *Tyler, Heather, Adam, and Jose*

Tyler and Heather had two children. One was in fourth grade, whereas the other was a high school senior. Tyler and Heather were quite happy with their children Adam (fourth grader) and Jose (high school senior). They would spend substantial quality time with them. They had breakfast and dinner with them. Adam and Jose had joyful playtimes and games with their father Tyler. Adam continued with this routine, but Jose got overly involved in using technology, playing video games, and watching television. Due to his changes in routine, he was not spending time with his parents. He also had bad experiences with his peers. He did not have time to discuss it with his parents. Tyler and Heather ignored it because they thought Jose was just exploring his identity and wanted some additional autonomy and independence. However, such an unhealthy routine affected Jose's sleeping and eating habits, and he started showing symptoms of depression. When his parents observed Jose's situation, they reacted quickly, sat with him, and discovered his situation. Both parents told him that he would be fine and it was just a matter of changing his routine. Tyler and Heather worked together, spending time with Jose, encouraged Adam to help and support his brother in adopting his previous routine with them. Over time, Jose started getting better, he decreased his screen time, left his peers who were stressing him out, and recovered from his depressive symptoms. The entire family came back to their routine when all the family members were spending sufficient time with each other, playing, and communicating with one another.

Moral of the Story

Parents are a big support for their children

What is your story? Write your story below:

_____
_____
_____
_____
_____
_____
_____
_____
_____
_____
_____

Activity

Meet with two students, read the above story before them, and ask about their parents' role in their life. Discover how parents provide them with their support, which ensures their growth and development. Compare the similarities and differences in parents' roles and support in raising their children.

Discussion Questions

1. What is the role of parents in children's lives?
2. How do parents support their children?
3. Why is parents' regular communication with their children important?
4. Why is parents' supervision of children important?
5. How do parents ensure their children's growth and development?

Chapter 21: Qualities of Supportive Societies

This chapter highlights that successful societies give priority to their citizens. They become quite sensitive in understanding the needs and experiences of their citizens. Not only do they understand their citizens, they also support them in addressing their needs so that their citizens can function effectively in society and become productive for themselves as well as for the society.

Quote

"Great societies on the earth feel the experiences of their citizens and support them accordingly to maximize their potential for themselves and society"

Description of Quote

The quote demonstrates that progressive and successful societies give priority to their citizens. They understand the experiences of their citizens and address their needs accordingly. Their goal is to support their citizens' growth to improve their potential and make them productive citizens of society.

What is your description of this quote? Write your description below:

_____

_____

_____

_____

_____

_____

_____

_____

_____

_____

_____

Story of Quote

CHARACTERS: Kelly and Joan

Kelly and Joan successfully completed their high school with very high grades. However, they did not have the finances to continue their college education. Both friends were quite eager to continue their higher education and do something special in their professional field for their fellow citizens and country. They kept trying and applying for different scholarships and funding, but it did not work. Once they met with the president of their local university in a conference. They took this opportunity and introduced themselves before the president. They shared their academic grades and told the president about their interest and willingness to continue their higher education. The president understood their situation and needs. He took a month and asked them to visit the university again. The president worked hard, consulted with state government and other stakeholder groups who collaborated and produced additional scholarships. The university also decreased the tuition for local students and also provided additional facilities and financial support to help students succeed. When Kelly and Joan visited the university and met with the president, they learned about all these updates and accomplishments that the president did in one month. Their happiness was beyond limit. The university gave scholarships to Kelly and Joan. Both were very excited since they knew they would continue their higher education and make a difference in their society.

Moral of the Story

Society and people work together to succeed

What is your story? Write your story below:

_____

_____

_____

_____

_____

_____

_____

_____

_____

_____

_____

Activity

Reach out to a few current students and read the above story with them. Ask about current challenges for students and their suggestions to address those challenges. Ask them to identify those actors who can play an important role in making essential changes in that regard.

Discussion Questions

1. Why is understanding people's experiences important?

2. How can societies support their citizens?

3. Why is it essential for citizens to live to their full potential?

4. How can people's potential be maximized?

5. How are productive citizens beneficial for their society?

Chapter 22: Knowledge, Application, and Practice

This chapter shows the importance of practice and experiential learning in addition to acquiring knowledge of specific contents. When people practice the knowledge they learn, they gain real-life experiences and make important networks interpersonally and professionally, which become quite useful for them in exploring their career and finding a job in a specific profession.

Quote

"Knowledge, practice, and experience are essential elements of learning"

Description of Quote

The quote demonstrates the importance of applying, reflecting on, and practicing classroom knowledge to foster and grow students' positive learning experiences. Students' learning is improved when they are facilitated by the instructor through various modalities to apply, reflect on, and practice the knowledge they learn in a classroom.

What is your description of this quote? Write your description below:

_____
_____
_____
_____
_____
_____
_____

Story of Quote

CHARACTERS: *Dr. Raza*

Students in higher education need opportunities to apply, reflect, and practice the knowledge that they learn in their classroom. Students learn in Dr. Raza's class because not only do they learn the course contents through various modalities, but they also have many different opportunities to apply, reflect, and practice the course contents. For instance, students write in their personal reflective journal that helps them to apply the course contents and reflect on their personal experiences. These personal reflective journals help students to assess their situations and determine where they would like to go in relation to the topic. Students also conduct small group discussions during which they share their personal experiences with each other and reflect on them, which fosters critical thinking and understanding of the topic personally and interpersonally. Students also work together in small groups and complete their service-learning projects, which provides them with essential opportunities to practice the knowledge they learn in real-life situations. Students work with different groups in diverse settings, such as school, family, community, and workplace to address their needs and provide them with appropriate solutions to their problems. Hence, in Dr. Raza's class students' positive learning experiences are grown and fostered through application, reflection, and practice.

Moral of the Story

Students learn through application, reflection, and practice

What is your story? Write your story below:

_____
_____
_____
_____
_____
_____
_____

Activity

Meet with a few students and discover what they have been learning in their classroom. Read the above story with them and ask them to focus on one specific topic. Then ask them to apply, reflect on, and practice the topic they mentioned. Examine their strengths and difficulties in applying, reflecting on, and practicing the topic.

Discussion Questions

1. Why is the application of knowledge important in learning?

2. Describe the benefits of the application of knowledge.

3. What are the ways to practice classroom knowledge?

4. How do people reflect on their personal experiences with respect to the topic?

5. How do application, reflection, and practice foster student learning experiences?

Chapter 23: Friendship and Continuity

This chapter shares the importance of friends in people's lives. Friends are a source of entertainment, happiness, and excitement for people. People share their private information with their friends without feeling any formality. Hence, people want to have friends and when they have friends, they need to make efforts to sustain their friend relationships.

Quote

"Friends are like a pleasant journey that people wish to continue"

Description of Quote

The quote shares the wealth of friendship. It shows that friends are a wealth that does not end but grows with positive interactions and relationships. People want to spend their substantial time in the pleasant company of their friends, and they want it to be continued over time.

What is your description of this quote? Write your description below:

_____
_____
_____
_____
_____
_____
_____
_____
_____
_____

Story of Quote

CHARACTERS: Jeremy and Megan

Jeremy and Megan were best friends from high school. They felt that each other was like supreme wealth they both were building by making positive interactions and showing respectful and trustworthy behaviors with each other. They were providing each other with social and emotional support. Additionally, they were also helping each other instrumentally. For instance, doing each other's household work, driving each other to the places when there was no transportation, and soothing each other when they were stressed and overwhelmed. Consequently, they were supporting each other's development. After some time, they decided to take admission to the same college and pursue a major in psychology. They both prepared for admission to meet the school's requirements and successfully secured their admission to an undergraduate degree in clinical psychology. As a result, they continued their friendship journey for a longer period of time with support, respect, and trust.

Moral of the Story

Friends are a supreme wealth for people

What is your story? Write your story below:

Activity

Meet with students who are each other's best friends. Read the above story with them. Ask them the value and importance of their friends. Ask them the reasons they would like to stay with their friends and continue such a pleasant journey with them.

Discussion Questions

1. What is friendship?

2. Why is friendship important for people?

3. How should people build their friendships?

4. How do friendships support and grow each other?

5. What are the important elements that foster a successful friendship?

Chapter 24: Importance of Culture

This chapter demonstrates the importance of positive traditions in ensuring the sustainability of one's culture. People value their culture because they make sense of the world based on their cultural values, beliefs, and perceptions. Hence, it is important for them to sustain their culture, and positive traditions are one of the essential ways to sustain a culture.

Quote

"Positive traditions ensure cultural sustainability"

Description of Quote

The quote highlights the significance of positive traditions for cultural groups. Due to globalization, it is essential for societies to preserve their original culture to a certain degree to ensure its sustainability. Hence, positive traditions maintain a continuity in cultural practices and guarantee cultural sustainability.

What is your description of this quote? Write your description below:

_____
_____
_____
_____
_____
_____
_____
_____
_____

Story of Quote

CHARACTERS: Linda, Gloria, and Sophia

Linda was a grandmother who was raising two grandchildren, Gloria and Sophia. Since they moved to the United States, both grandchildren were forgetting and ignoring their culture of origin and frequently adopting the US culture. Both grandchildren were teenagers, so they were exploring their identities and wanting to have autonomy. Linda thought that although it was a good thing for both children to familiarize themselves with the US culture, they also need to preserve and maintain their culture of origin. Keeping in mind the importance of their original culture, the ages of her grandchildren, and the strong influences of the current culture, Linda started celebrating their cultural traditions from time to time in the family. For instance, she would cook specific cultural food for her grandchildren, bought paintings that reflected their cultural practices, and she talked in their native language. She also kept telling the significance of these traditions and cultural symbols to her children. Over time, without any arguments or interruption, her grandchildren preserved and maintained their culture of origin along with the US culture. They were quite proud of their situation and what they had in terms of their culture. Linda supported her grandchildren in maintaining a good and healthy balance between the US culture and their culture of origin.

Moral of the Story

Balancing two cultures in a healthy manner

What is your story? Write your story below:

_____

_____

_____

_____

_____

_____

_____

_____

_____

_____

Activity

Meet with a few students whose native language and culture of origin are different than the US culture. Read the above story with them and discover how they are maintaining a healthy balance between their culture of origin and the US culture to preserve and maintain their culture of origin.

Discussion Questions

1. Why is culture of origin important?

2. What are some ways individuals and families preserve their culture of origin?

3. Why is it important to adapt to the current culture in a different country?

4. How do people find a healthy balance between the current country's culture and their culture of origin?

5. What are the benefits of maintaining a healthy balance between the current country's culture and their culture of origin?

Chapter 25: Parent-Child Love and Affection

This chapter demonstrates the durability of the parent-child relationship as they always stay throughout the life span. When children are young, they receive love and care from their parents because they are more dependent on their parents, and when they become adults and their parents get older, their parents receive more love and care from their children. Hence, the nature of parent-child love and relationship change over time.

Quote

"Parent-child love and relationship do not end as children grow, the nature of it is changed"

Description of Quote

The quote shows the dynamics of parent-child relationships and how they change over time as children grow and become adults. When children are younger, they are more dependent on parents. Both parent and child love each other; however, parents are like a guide for children and more influential in the relationship. When parents get older and their adult children support and care for them, though the dynamics of the parent-child relationship are changed, they still love one another.

What is your description of this quote? Write your description below:

_____

_____

_____

_____

_____

_____

_____

_____

_____

_____

_____

Story of Quote

CHARACTERS: Bryan, Ann, and Kathryn

Bryan raised his two daughters, Ann and Kathryn, quite well. Ann and Kathryn had their families with children. When Ann and Kathryn were young, Bryan worked hard to build a healthy attachment with his children. He was quite sensitive in dividing his time between his young children, understanding their experiences with care and sensitivity, and addressing their needs adequately. Now, since Bryan is in the elderly period, the nature of their relationship has changed. Bryan needs more care, affection, and love from Ann and Kathryn. They still share positive and healthy attachments with one another; the direction and nature of their love and relationship has changed. Ann and Kathryn realize that when they were children, they were vulnerable and dependent on their father, who provided them with substantial love, care, and affection. This is the time when he is weak, sensitive, and needs them to connect with him and help him understand that he is a successful person who prepared his children to perform well and survive in contemporary and tough society. Hence, the relationship between Bryan, Ann, and Kathryn did not change over time in terms of love and affection, the nature and direction of it was changed.

Moral of the Story

Parent-child love and affection stay over time

What is your story? Write your story below:

_____

_____

_____

_____

_____

_____

_____

_____

_____

_____

_____

Activity

Meet with an adult who has at least one elderly parent and young children and share the above story with them. Learn about their love and relationship with their parents, how it has changed, and whether they have the same degree of love with one another.

Discussion Questions

1. What is a parent-child relationship?

2. Discuss the dynamics of parent-child relationships.

3. How does the parent-child relationship change when children become adults?

4. Discuss the degree of love between parents and children.

5. Discuss whether love changes between parents and children when adult children have their own children.

Chapter 26: Love and Expressions

This chapter shares the linkages between love and the lover's expression of love for the person whom they love. When they express their love, they express the person whom they love and when they express the person, they express them with love and affection. Hence, either way, their expression centers around the person whom they love.

Quote

"When I express love, you are expressed, and when I express you, love is expressed"

Description of Quote

The quote promotes love, romance, and affection between lovers. When a person falls in love with someone, their conversations revolve around that person. Their expressions are full of the qualities of the one they love. Hence, love, expression, and the person become intertwined with one another.

What is your description of this quote? Write your description below:
_____
_____
_____
_____
_____
_____
_____
_____
_____

Story of Quote

CHARACTERS: Juan and Amber

Juan and Amber fell in love with one another. Juan was very expressive because he was a poet. After falling in love with Amber, his poetry substantially changed because whenever he was writing something, he was imagining Amber into his eyes and mind. He was feeling Amber in his heart, which was reflected in his words and poetry. Hence, all his written expressions belonged to her. Whenever he would meet with Amber, he was quite excited. Since he was a poet, he had the power of writing, he felt the moment and expressed it through his poetry. For instance, he was expressing Amber's beauty, her smile, the way she was talking, walking, and arguing in his poetry. He was expressing Amber with love, affection, and emotion. Hence, all his poetry and written expressions were revolving around Amber, whom he fell in love with.

Moral of the Story

Expressions of love are linked to the person who is loved

What is your story? Write your story below:

Activity

Meet with a couple who fall in love with one another, share the above story with them, and ask the degree to which they relate to the story. Discover their opinion on how the expression of love is linked with that person who they love.

Discussion Questions

1. What is an expression of love?

2. Why is an expression important in love?

3. How do people's conversations revolve around whom they love?

4. How are love, expression, and person linked with each other in love?

5. How do couples promote love and expression in their relationship?

Chapter 27: Evening Is a Productive Time

This chapter presents the importance of the evening for couples and families. It describes that the evening is a useful time for couples and families to spend some time together, ask about daily routines, and support each other in that routine. It is a time that couples and families can effectively utilize to work on any problems to resolve them and build healthy couple and family relationships.

Quote

"Evening is a good time for a couple to connect with each other, reflect on the day, and work on their relationship"

Description of Quote

The quote highlights the importance of the evening for couples and how couples can effectively utilize the evening for different purposes and needs. Couples can learn about each other's day to connect with one another, they can discuss any unresolved issue and find appropriate solutions, share plans, and work together in building their relationship. Hence, when couples are thoughtful about their evening, they are more likely to constructively use it and build a healthy couple relationship.

_____

_____

_____

_____

_____

_____

_____
_____
_____
_____
_____

Story of Quote

CHARACTERS: Brian and Erin

Brian and Erin were husband and wife. Since both were working full time, due to their busy routines they were not able to spend substantial time with one another. Consequently, their relationship was affected. Suddenly, Erin thought that, though they could not spend their daytime with each other, they could still have the evening to talk to one another. Rather than getting involved with television, cell phones, or the computer, they could connect with one another after work, ask about each other's day, and work on their relationship problems. She discussed this idea with Brian who delightedly agreed to work on it. First, they started light conversations and spent some time with each other to reconnect and preserve the same degree of relationship. Then they used their strengths, such as support and communication, to further build their relationship and work together to resolve their relationship issues. They were so excited and delighted with how they effectively utilized the evening to rebuild their relationship and prevent themselves from facing any separation. They made evening their best time and never left such a wonderful opportunity in their entire life.

Moral of the Story

Evening is the best time for couples to reconnect with one another

What is your story? Write your story below:

_____
_____
_____
_____
_____
_____

Activity

Reach out to a couple, share the above story with them, and discover how they utilize their evening. Ask whether the story opens ways for them to further effectively utilize their evening in building their relationship.

Discussion Questions

1. Why is the evening important for couples?
2. How can couples effectively utilize their evening?
3. What aspects of life can a couple focus on during the evening?
4. How can couples work together in building their relationship during the evening?
5. How can couples be prepared in effectively utilizing their evening?

Chapter 28: The Power of Writing

This chapter highlights the power and influence of writers and writing. Writers share many useful ideas, suggestions, and plans with their readers to initiate and maintain different hobbies, pursue any goals, and carry out certain activities. Hence, they promote people's interest and critical thinking in many areas of their lives. When people find their ideas relevant and closer to their life, they become interested in those ideas and are more likely to follow them.

Quote

"Writers promote interest, critical thinking, and relevance among readers"

Description of Quote

The quote describes the quality of writers who play an important role in promoting people's interest in many areas and motivate people to pursue those interests by sharing their advantages. Their writings provide people with opportunities to critically think about any topic or phenomenon shared in a particular writing piece. When people find writing useful, meaningful, and relevant to their lives, writers, written pieces, and writing itself fascinate them.

What is your description of this quote? Write your description below:

_____
_____
_____
_____
_____

_____
_____
_____
_____
_____
_____

Story of Quote

CHARACTERS: Hussain

Hussain is a writer who uses his writing abilities and critical thinking to share and introduce different fun activities, games, and hobbies among his readers. Sometimes, it happens that people do not know about certain simple hobbies and activities, such as reading a book, writing journals, and mindfulness and the positive impact of these things on their lives. When they learn about these things, it promotes their interest. They become more sensitive and thoughtful in carrying out their daily routines. Hussain also is sensitive to the age groups of his audiences. Hence, he categorizes his suggestions based on each age group to grow and foster relevance among his readers. When his audiences find these fun activities, games, and hobbies according to their age, they get more interested due to their relevance and significance. Hence, by using the power of writing, Hussain has been promoting healthy lifestyles and routines among his audiences.

Moral of the Story

Writing is a benefit in promoting healthy lifestyles among people

What is your story? Write your story below:

_____
_____
_____
_____
_____
_____
_____
_____

Activity

Reach out to a few individuals, share the above story, and learn about their interest in reading and writing. Ask about their opinions in how writers play an important role in promoting people's interest, critical thinking, and relevance among readers.

Discussion Questions

1. What are the qualities of good writers?
2. How does writing promote critical thinking among readers?
3. How do people promote reading and writing among others?
4. How does writing promote people's interest?
5. Why does a written piece need to be relevant and meaningful for readers?

Chapter 29: Creative Work, Appreciation, and Economic Value

This chapter demonstrates that innovation and creative work are essential elements of successful societies. Successful societies promote creative work and bring it into the mainstream of society to associate an economic value to it. Consequently, people get economic benefits when they create new ideas or things. This further increases their growth and development of such work because people don't feel scared; rather, they get excited because they know that their efforts toward creating new and unique work will pay off.

Quote

"When societies promote creative work and associate economic value to it, it fosters the growth of such work"

Description of Quote

The quote shows the importance of societal support for creative work. Creative work is highly important for all societies because it supports the advancement of knowledge, skills, and innovation. Hence, societies need to promote it among their citizens. An economic value of such work also increases people's motivation to become creative and produce such work. Consequently, such promotions and motivations regarding creative work ensure its growth and development in those societies.

What is your description of this quote? Write your description below:

_____

_____

_____
_____
_____
_____
_____
_____
_____
_____
_____

Story of Quote

CHARACTERS: Ali

Ali was very creative since his childhood. He developed software, programs, and other advanced technological tools. In his country, there was no value and appreciation of his work. His parents supported him in his work but because he was not receiving any scholarship or funding from any government or nongovernment sources, it was quite difficult for him to continue his research and discovery. One day, one of his friends suggested he explore US schools and contact them for scholarship and funding. He understood that if he would like to continue his research and discovery, he needed financial assistance and institutional support. Consequently, he started contacting US universities and sharing his products and ideas with them. In no time, he received many scholarship offers from which he chose one. Due to financial assistance and institutional support, he made substantial contributions and advancement in his field. He is now one of the leaders and mentors in his professional field.

Moral of the Story

Creative work sells itself

What is your story? Write your story below:

_____
_____
_____
_____

_____

_____

_____

_____

_____

_____

Activity

Reach out to a group of youths, share the above story, and ask their opinion about creative work. Discover their suggestions to promote creative work. Ask if they ever did any creative work and the outcome of it.

Discussion Questions

1. What is creative work?

2. Why is creative work important for building new knowledge?

3. How do societies promote creative work among their citizens?

4. What are the motivational factors to promote creative work?

5. What are the challenges and opportunities in creative work?

Chapter 30: People's Real-Life Experiences

This chapter illustrates that people's real-life experiences are important to understand their life. People are different from one another. Their life experiences and stories are also unique and different from each other. Hence, in order to understand their lives, it is important to learn about their personal experiences.

Quote

"The truth of life lies in people's lives"

Description of Quote

The quote demonstrates the significance of people's real-life experiences. People's lived experiences show their life and its reality. Hence, in order to learn about people's lives, it is essential to learn about their real-life and lived experiences.

What is your description of this quote? Write your description below:

_____
_____
_____
_____
_____
_____
_____
_____
_____
_____

Story of Quote

CHARACTERS: Rasti

Rasti grew up in a wealthy family. She was living a luxurious life. She got everything before time. She was happy and excited in her life. However, she never thought about those people who struggled to meet their basic needs such as food, shelter, and clothes. One day she decided to visit homeless people to learn about their lives and experiences. It was quite a distressful time for her when she observed their situations and talked to them. She learned how they were struggling to meet their basic needs. This one day changed her life and she decided to run a nongovernment organization to support homeless and needy people for meeting their basic needs. She allocated substantial funds from her personal wealth and also contacted many donor agencies that gave her sufficient funds to develop and carry out effective programs to support needy and homeless people. She was always thankful for that day when she went to learn about other people's real-life situations and experiences, which changed her entire thinking and life.

Moral of the Story

People's real-life experiences are central to life

What is your story? Write your story below:

_____
_____
_____
_____
_____
_____
_____
_____
_____
_____
_____

Activity

Reach out to an individual and share the above story with them. Learn about their real-life experiences and how these experiences shaped their entire life. Reflect on your conversation with them to discover why people's lived experiences which reveal their life and its realities are important.

Discussion Questions

1. What are people's real-life experiences?

2. Why are real-life experiences important in people's lives?

3. How do people's lives lie in their real-life experiences?

4. How do people's lived experiences shape their lives?

5. Why is it important to learn about people's experiences to discover their life?

Chapter 31: Spirituality and Compassion

This chapter discusses spirituality and how spirituality provides people with positive thinking and compassion and creates a willingness to sacrifice for others. Additionally, spirituality also prevents people from being self-centered. People become spiritual when they love, help, and support others.

Quote

"Spirituality enlightens people with positive thinking to become more sacrificing for others and avoid any self-centeredness"

Description of Quote

The quote shares the qualities of spirituality that discourages self-centeredness and encourages compassion and empathy for others. People promote positive thinking when they become spiritual. They find a peace of mind and a purpose in life when they help others. They prioritize others' needs over their own needs. Consequently, they are ready to sacrifice to address others' needs and make them happy, which grows them spiritually.

What is your description of this quote? Write your description below:

_____
_____
_____
_____
_____
_____
_____
_____

_____
_____
_____

Story of Quote

CHARACTERS: Tyler

Tyler was eager to learn and practice spirituality. He kept reading books, attending spiritual events, and watching different videos and shows on spirituality. After spending extensive time learning about spirituality, he discovered that he needed to promote positive thinking about others in himself. According to him, spirituality was about showing compassion and sacrificing for others. Spirituality promotes positive thinking about others and prevents people from becoming self-centered. After learning about spirituality, Tyler joined many community organizations and started working as a volunteer. His goal was to help and support people. So, he was not missing any opportunities to work with people and support them. He was also saving money from his earnings and giving it as a donation to help homeless people. All this work made him more spiritual. He was quite satisfied, content, and happy with his life and routines.

Moral of the Story

Spirituality increases positivity

What is your story? Write your story below:

_____
_____
_____
_____
_____
_____
_____
_____
_____
_____
_____

Activity

Reach out to a few people, read the above story, and ask them how they feel when they help others. Discover their feelings when they become sacrificing and compassionate for others and avoid self-centeredness. Ask them how much such positive thinking is beneficial for others as well as themselves.

Discussion Questions

1. What is spirituality?
2. How does spirituality promote positive thinking among people?
3. How do spiritual people become more sacrificing?
4. How does spirituality promote empathy and compassion for people?
5. Why do spiritual people avoid self-centeredness?

Chapter 32: Sustainable Efforts and Long-Term Solutions

This chapter presents sustainability and the challenges and rewards associated with it. Though sustainability is difficult, and when people carry out sustainable actions they face many challenges, sustainability resolves people's problems for an extended period of time, which means that the rewards of sustainability pay off its cost quite well.

Quote

"Sustainable efforts bring tough situations for people, but they address people's important problems on a long-term basis"

Description of Quote

The quote highlights that sustainability is difficult and sustainable efforts are tough because they bring all potential stakeholder groups together to address important problems. Sustainable actions also create tough situations and challenges because sometimes the entire structure needs to be changed or built from scratch to support such efforts. However, sustainable efforts provide long-term solutions to current problems. Hence, when people want to have permanent solutions to their problems, they need to carry out sustainable efforts.

What is your description of this quote? Write your description below:

_____
_____
_____
_____

Story of Quote

CHARACTERS: Adam, Peter, and Walter

Adam, Peter, and Walter were living in a community which was experiencing severe poverty. They were best friends and quite concerned about the situation of the community since it was very difficult for most of the families to meet their basic needs. They applied for and received a few grants, but those funds did not provide them with a sustainable solution. They kept thinking and planning ideas on how to bring sustainable changes and solutions to their community. Then they figured out that until the community people worked together and focused on these issues, they may not fix poverty for a long time. People knew the problems and they must provide the solutions. They made extensive efforts to gather and motivate people, but all efforts failed to convince people at the beginning. Slowly and steadily, people started listening to them and becoming a part of their campaign. They registered with a local organization for their community and people started giving funds to that organization. They developed a program with the consultation of community people through which they offered occupational training and small business development to community people. Rich people within and outside of the community were financially participating in that program. Over time, they were able to increase the employment rates since many people started working, and decrease poverty as people were making money from their businesses. They also made connections outside of the community, selling their community's products and services. The entire community's condition substantially changed after some time and this positive change was quite sustainable and long term.

Moral of the Story

Sustainable actions are tough and challenging

What is your story? Write your story below:

_____
_____
_____
_____
_____
_____
_____
_____
_____
_____
_____
_____

Activity

Reach out to a few students and read the above story with them. Ask about their ideas and views about sustainability. Ask about why sustainable efforts are important for the success and sustainability of society.

Discussion Questions

1. What is sustainability?

2. Why are sustainable efforts important for the success and sustainability of society?

3. How does sustainability bring tough situations among people?

4. How does sustainability address important problems that people face?

5. How does sustainability provide long-term solutions to current problems?

Chapter 33: Children's Trust and Sleep Quality

This chapter shares the importance of building trust between parents and children, especially when children are young. When children are young, their parents make an important impact on them. Thus, when a primary caregiver develops trust in a child and the child experiences that trust, they feel better during the day and sleep well at night.

Quote

"Children experience a greater sleep quality when they build trust in their parents"

Description of Quote

The quote guides parents to build trust in their children. When children are younger, they are more vulnerable and dependent on their parents. Parents have more influence on their children. For instance, when parents behave with care and sensitivity, their children feel excited and build trust in their parents. Due to this trust, they feel protected, which helps them to experience a greater sleep quality.

What is your description of this quote? Write your description below:

_____

_____

_____

_____

_____

_____

_____
_____
_____
_____
_____

Story of Quote

CHARACTERS: Julia and Juan

Julia had a new baby, Juan. At the beginning, the newborn was not quite comfortable, crying and showing restlessness and discomfort. Julia tried to comfort Juan, but her efforts were not quite useful in comforting Juan. Consequently, Juan was not sleeping the whole night; instead, he was crying and showing discomfort even in Julia's presence. Then Julia contacted a therapist who advised Julia to show sensitivity and compassion in raising her child after listening to her. He further told her to build trust with her child. Julia showed additional sensitivity and understanding of the needs of her child. She was also quite responsive to the needs of her child. She was also spending more time with her child to comfort him. Consequently, she was able to build trust in her child. After some time, she noticed that her child was having a deep and peaceful sleep every night. She was happy about her child and the overall situation.

Moral of the Story

Children's trust in their primary caregiver makes a big difference in their sleep quality

What is your story? Write your story below:

_____
_____
_____
_____
_____
_____
_____
_____
_____

Activity

Reach out to a few teenagers and read the above story with them. Ask about their views and ideas on building trust between parents and children and how it promotes a greater sleep quality for children. Discover their childhood experiences about it.

Discussion Questions

1. What is sleep quality?
2. How does parent-child trust promote greater sleep quality?
3. How do parents build trust in their children?
4. Why are trust and sleep important for young children?
5. How do parents learn to build trust in their children?

Chapter 34: Meaning of Spirituality

This chapter discusses the practice and meaning of spirituality and how people make meaning of spirituality and practice it differently. Spirituality is a more individualized aspect of people's lives. For instance, some people just focus on themselves, become humble, and connect with divine forces, others work with people to support them, whereas another group of people may combine these two aspects because that's what spirituality means to them. Hence, people's meanings and practices of spirituality vary.

Quote

"The practice and meaning of spirituality vary among people"

Description of Quote

The quote illustrates that spirituality is more an individualized aspect of people's life. People's meaning of spirituality is different from one another. Consequently, the way people practice spirituality is also different. For instance, some people may want to focus on themselves and work to make stronger connections with divine forces to become spiritual, whereas other people want to support and help others to find the purpose of their life and to become spiritual. Hence, the practice and meaning of spirituality vary among people.

What is your description of this quote? Write your description below:

_____

_____

_____

_____

_____
_____
_____
_____
_____
_____
_____

Story of Quote

CHARACTERS: Albert and Diana

Albert and Diana were both practicing spirituality. However, their meaning and practice of spirituality were different from one another. Albert was involved in understanding himself and making connections with the divine forces, because for him, spirituality was about the purity of heart and soul. He believed in his reflective practices, selflessness, and humbleness, which made his connection stronger with himself and the divine forces. In contrast, for Diana, spirituality was more about making connections with people, understanding their experiences, and supporting them to meet their basic needs. Consequently, she was donating a lot of money from her pocket for this purpose. Additionally, she was also working in her local community to help and support people in their lives. Her meaning of spirituality was to make people happy, and she was practicing it quite efficiently. Hence, both Albert and Diana were quite happy and satisfied with their lives. They both were practicing spirituality. However, their meaning and practice of spirituality was different from one another.

Moral of the Story

Spirituality has an individualized aspect for people

What is your story? Write your story below:

_____
_____
_____
_____
_____

_____

_____

_____

_____

_____

Activity

Reach out to a few people and read the above story with them. Discover their meaning of spirituality. Ask them how they practice spirituality. Compare the meaning and practice of spirituality between them.

Discussion Questions

1. How do people vary in their spirituality with one another?
2. What meaning do people make of spirituality?
3. What are the ways people practice spirituality?
4. How do different practices belong to spirituality?
5. How do spiritual practices relate to one another?

Chapter 35: People's Interest and Innovation

This chapter shares the significance of promoting and encouraging people's interest in specific areas that they like and want to work on. When people like what they do, they dive into the depth of knowledge, acquire new skills, and practice new ways of doing things, which promotes discovery and innovation in those areas and fields.

Quote

"People's interest in specific areas promotes discovery and innovation in those areas"

Description of Quote

The quote shows when people are interested in a specific area, they want to learn more about that area, get additional expertise, take risks, and go to a much deeper level. Consequently, it promotes research, discovery, and innovation in that area. Hence, it is important to support and facilitate people in those areas in which they are interested in working.

What is your description of this quote? Write your description below:

_____
_____
_____
_____
_____
_____
_____

_____
_____
_____
_____

Story of Quote

CHARACTERS: Lucas, Roy, and Brittany

Lucas wanted to become a computer engineer, but his father, Roy, wanted him to become a doctor. Lucas tried his best to convince Roy, but it was quite difficult to convince him. Then his mother, Brittany, sat down with her husband and explained to him that their son had an interest in computer science and not in medicine. If he agreed to pursue medicine, he would not do well in that field because he did not have any interest in medicine. After several meetings, Roy was convinced and he supported Lucas to get a master's in computer science. He was so passionate about his work. Consequently, he dived deeper into the knowledge and acquired substantial skills. His supervisor also noticed his abilities and further promoted his work in his area of specialization. He made substantial innovations and discoveries in his field during his internship. While he was doing his internship, he was offered a job from a multinational company as a software developer. He was so excited about it. When he told this news to his parents, their joy and excitement were beyond the limits. His father was quite happy and satisfied with his decision. Lucas started a successful career, and his parents were so proud of him.

Moral of the Story

People's interest has a value for their work

What is your story? Write your story below:

_____
_____
_____
_____
_____
_____

_____

_____

_____

_____

Activity

Reach out to a few students and read the above story with them. Ask about their interest in their studies and profession. Discover from them how deeply they want to work in their area of interest compared to those areas in which they lack interest.

Discussion Questions

1. Why is people's interest in their profession important?

2. How do people explore and discover their interest in a profession?

3. How do people's interest in a certain area motivate them to work harder?

4. How do people's interest promote discovery and innovation?

5. How should employers promote and facilitate employees' interest in the workplace?

Chapter 36: Leadership Influences

This chapter demonstrates the importance of successful leadership and the impact of leaders' words among their followers. Leaders are mindful, critical, and thoughtful who pass those statements on and share views that encourage their followers to critically think about the situations they face, assess those situations, and reflect on their experiences, which also makes them critical thinkers and promotes leadership qualities among them.

Quote

"Leaders' words promote reflection and critical thinking among their people"

Description of Quote

This quote highlights the importance of leaders' words and statements for their people. Successful leaders are critical and transformative. Hence, their goal is to promote critical thinking and self-reflection among their people so that they can understand their issues and find appropriate solutions to those problems, and to grow and develop over time.

What is your description of this quote? Write your description below:

_____
_____
_____
_____
_____
_____
_____

_____
_____
_____
_____

Story of Quote

CHARACTERS: Randy

Randy was a successful community leader. He always connected with the community members who were following him and following his agenda for community change. Since he knew his community and its people very closely, his conversations were always promoting critical thinking and reflection among his followers. For instance, the community was facing a shortage of teachers in local schools. His conversations were highlighting this issue among his people. He was also targeting the youth and motivating them to become teachers. He was also inviting successful teachers from the local schools to community events where they were sharing their passion for teaching and success stories with community people. Consequently, the youth started thinking about and choosing teaching as a profession. Simultaneously, Randy also worked with school district and state officials to increase funds and scholarships for prospective teachers. Due to all these efforts, there was a steady increase in teachers at local schools.

Moral of the Story

Leaders bring positive changes in the lives of their people

What is your story? Write your story below:

_____
_____
_____
_____
_____
_____
_____
_____

Activity

Reach out to a few people and read the above story with them. Ask about the qualities of leadership. Discover the importance of a leader's words for their followers. Ask about the need for leadership in contemporary societies. Are the current leaders performing their roles effectively?

Discussion Questions

1. Who are the leaders?
2. Why are leaders important for society?
3. What roles do leaders play in society?
4. What is the significance of a leader's words and statements for their followers?
5. How do leaders' words promote critical thinking and reflection among their followers?

Chapter 37: Aging Populations and Contemporary Society

This chapter shares that the aging population is important and functional for society. Though they face some challenges due to their age-specific changes and becoming more vulnerable to experiencing chronic illness, they can still play an important role in the prosperity and development of society. However, they need additional support from different domains of society, such as the family, community, social, economic, and political domains to increase their opportunities and decrease their challenges.

Quote

"Aging populations need additional support from society to expand opportunities and minimize challenges for themselves"

Description of Quote

This quote shows that in the current society aging populations are substantially growing. This group of the population has special needs because they are in their elderly period. Hence, they need additional support from society and people around them to minimize their challenges and maximize their opportunities.

What is your description of this quote? Write your description below:

_____
_____
_____
_____
_____

_____
_____
_____
_____
_____
_____

Story of Quote

CHARACTERS: Logan

Logan was running a nongovernment organization, and its focus was on community development. He was getting older and experiencing age-specific changes. He also understood that his needs were different at this age compared to when he was young. He started talking to elderly people in his community. He was directly and indirectly observing them. Over time, he found out that elderly people have the potential to contribute to the community. However, someone needed to facilitate this group of the population to expand their opportunities and minimize their challenges. Consequently, he offered volunteer opportunities through his organization where elderly people could engage and serve the community. He also created an elderly social network where elderly people could meet with each other, make connections, and support one another in their lives. One of his projects was also approved for funding that focused on developing the neighborhood so that elderly people could walk and perform their daily activities smoothly. Consequently, he expanded the opportunities and minimized the challenges for elderly people who were quite delighted and satisfied to make their important contribution to community development.

Moral of the Story

The elderly population makes a substantial contribution in communities

What is your story? Write your story below:

_____
_____
_____
_____

_____

_____

_____

_____

_____

_____

Activity

Reach out to a few elderly people and read the above story with them. Ask about their experiences in their neighborhood and society. Discover their challenges and opportunities. Ask about the support they need to minimize their challenges and maximize their opportunities.

Discussion Questions

1. What is aging?

2. Discuss the qualities of aging populations.

3. What challenges do they face in society?

4. What opportunities do they have in society?

5. What support do they need to function well in society?

Chapter 38: Love and Sustainable Relationships

This chapter highlights that successful and sustainable relationships are more likely to be built on love. When people love each other, form healthy relationships, and make concrete efforts to sustain them, it demonstrates the role of love in their relationships.

Quote

"Healthy and sustainable relationships are a legacy of love"

Description of Quote

The quote illustrates the significance of love in building sustainable and healthy relationships. Those relationships which are loving and healthy are grounded in love and continue over time in a positive manner.

What is your description of this quote? Write your description below:

_____
_____
_____
_____
_____
_____
_____
_____
_____
_____
_____
_____
_____

Story of Quote

CHARACTERS: Alan and Joe

Alan and Joe each had a family of two children and a wife. They were best friends since their childhood. They were living in the same neighborhood where they were supporting one another. They believed that friends are a big support for one another. Consequently, they also encouraged their children to build a healthy friendship and loving relationship with each other. Over time, their children also became one another's best friends. They were also observing their fathers and mothers who were collaborating with each other and supporting one another in day-to-day tasks and activities. When children grew up, they sustained that healthy relationship which they built in their children. Both families were a great support for each other. Due to having such social support, both families were effectively dealing with any expected or unexpected problems. The friend relationship which was developed on love by their parents paid off overtime for their children too.

Moral of the Story

Love is the foundation of every healthy relationship

What is your story? Write your story below:

_____

_____

_____

_____

_____

_____

_____

_____

_____

_____

_____

Activity

Reach out to a few young people and read the above story with them. Ask about their relationships with others. How did they build those relationships? Discover the role of love in building those relationships. How did love help them to sustain their relationships?

Discussion Questions

1. What are healthy relationships?
2. How do relationships become sustainable?
3. What is the role of love in building healthy relationships?
4. How does love sustain relationships with others?
5. Why is love important in relationships?

Chapter 39: Leadership Approaches

This chapter shares the characteristics of successful leadership. Successful leaders view their people's situations comprehensively and carry out holistic efforts to support all aspects of their lives. Their approaches come from people who actively participate in a decision-making process. Leaders are involved in people's lives quite regularly and actively, hence, they are well aware of the problems that their people face.

Quote

"Successful leadership is holistic and people-centered"

Description of Quote

The quote shows the qualities of successful leadership. Successful leaders critically examine all aspects of their people's lives and carry out appropriate actions, which benefit their people holistically. They prioritize their people's problems and needs, and their approaches are people-centered to address those problems and needs.

What is your description of this quote? Write your description below:

_____

_____

_____

_____

_____

_____

_____

_____

_____

_____

_____

Story of Quote

CHARACTERS: George

George was the CEO of his organization. He was the leader of all his employees who looked to him and tried to follow his agenda and directions. His leadership was quite comprehensive. He not only focused on one group of employees who were well-educated and skilled, but he included all employees regardless of their education and background in his programs and benefits. His programs facilitated employees in many aspects of the workplace, such as coworkers' support, supervisors' support, family-friendly workplace policies, mothers' friendly workplace environment, etc. Since he was so close to his employees, he understood their problems quite well. Consequently, his policies and programs were employee-centered, which addressed employees' needs and provided them with positive workplace experiences.

Moral of the Story

Contemporary leadership needs to be people-centered

What is your story? Write your story below:

_____

_____

_____

_____

_____

_____

_____

_____

_____

_____

_____

Activity

Reach out to a few people and read the above story with them. Ask about the approaches of leadership to transform their people's lives. Why are successful leaders comprehensive and clear in their approaches? Why are successful leaders people centered.

Discussion Questions

1. What is successful leadership?
2. How is successful leadership holistic?
3. What are leadership-successful approaches?
4. How do successful leaders be transformative?
5. Why are successful leaders people centered?

Chapter 40: Importance of Education and Educators

This chapter demonstrates that both education and educators are equally important in society because they support and promote each other. Education prepares educators to teach and mentor others, whereas educators spread education for the benefit of others. Hence, both education and educators support and substantiate each other.

Quote

"Education and educators are equally important because they substantiate each other"

Description of Quote

The quote highlights the importance of educators and education as they both are equally important and support one another. People gain education and become educators who educate, guide, and mentor others. Consequently, they spread education among others. When they spread education, they not only benefit others, but they also benefit themselves. Hence, both education and educators support each other.

What is your description of this quote? Write your description below:

_____
_____
_____
_____
_____
_____

_____
_____
_____
_____
_____

Story of Quote

CHARACTERS: Sarah

Sarah belonged to a poor family. She was so passionate about her education. Due to financial problems, she had to stop her education after completing high school. However, she did not lose heart and kept trying to get a scholarship. Due to her abilities in math and science, she received a full scholarship to become a math teacher. She performed quite well at all higher educational levels and successfully completed her doctorate in education. Her parents and all family members were so proud of her. She knew that she became an educator and received such respect from her loved ones due to her education. She devoted her life to spread education and prepare educators. She was also conducting research to highlight support for potential teachers. She was collaborating with others, attending conferences, and conducting workshops to promote education among people. Her education supported her to become an educator and being an educator, she was supporting others in their education and spreading education as much as she could.

Moral of the Story

Education always pays off

What is your story? Write your story below:

_____
_____
_____
_____
_____
_____
_____

Activity

Reach out to a few students who pursue an education degree and profession and read the above story with them. Ask about the importance of education for them in preparing them to be an educator. Being an educator, how can they spread education among others?

Discussion Questions

1. Why is education important?
2. Why are educators equally as important as education?
3. In what ways does education support educators?
4. How do educators support education?
5. What is the role of education and educators in a successful society?

One Thousand Quotes

Muhammad Hassan Raza

THIS SECOND PART OF the book contains one thousand unique quotes. These quotes are distinctive statements, which have never been said or written by anyone in the past. The quotes are grouped in seven different categories, which include Love and Romance, Family and Relationships, Friendship and Society, Science and Education, Leadership and Culture, Spirituality and Compassion, and Poetry and Writing. These quotes provide the audience with unique and new knowledge on various aspects of life. Readers can apply these quotes to their personal experiences and also reflect on these quotes to explore and discover additional benefits from them.

Love and Romance

"Love is about valuing the heart"

"Love is a complex form of friendship"

"Love is a blessing of blessed hearts"

"The heart is a symbol of love, whereas love signifies healthy relationships"

"When you look at their eyes and you see yourself in them, you stay in their heart because eyes show what the heart feels"

"A strong sense of observation is a core element of love because people become sensitive to and want to care for the one whom they love"

"Love is when you are alone but satisfied because you know you love them"

"Love is wealth which people don't earn, but they need to make substantial efforts to keep"

"Trust is when their one word is heavier than hundreds of words said by hundreds of people"

"When your observations become quite strong just because they are around you, they are quite special for you"

"Eyes and heart actively function for sending messages between people who are in love"

"Love enlightens the heart and soul, and people who are in love feel it"

"The first letter of love is a symbol for people that signifies living together"

"When a short meeting with them feels like more than a life, you are in love"

"When a silence tells the story of hearts between people, the signs of love grow"

"The heart and rose share an important quality that they both are a symbol of love; give your heart and a rose to your loved ones"

"Love is the desire to meet with the one whom you love"

"Love is a treasure for the heart and the heart finds it for itself"

"Two souls are usually two reflections, but love makes them one reflection"

"Love is charming and energetic"

"When people are around you, but you only see the one whom you love, you are in love"

"When you wait for them all night and don't feel tired, rather, you get excited to see them again in the morning, they become quite special for you"

"Love does not contain any doubt because it is crystal and pure"

"If they like you and you visit them, they will welcome you from their eyes"

"When they talk to you for a moment and you keep repeating what they say every moment, you are in love"

"Music, dance, and writing are essential elements of a healthy relationship"

"A long, stressful night becomes a pleasant morning when they come to your home, and you see their face"

"Love is about feeling in the heart and explaining it to one another"

"When the time before you meet them feels too long and the time of meeting them feels too short, you are in love"

"When souls meet, hearts get connected and the body experiences positive sensations, people are in love"

"When you find no one like the one, you are in love with them"

"When people are in love, their hearts are connected and their relationships become their reflection"

"People show the reflection of their heart when they demonstrate their love for other"

"When the heart creates a picture of their face that reflects through your eyes, you are in love"

"The conflict of love is the conflict of hearts between people"

"You make them happy, whom you love, and feel good even though you don't see them"

"The practice of love that people learn improves its value to a greater degree"

"When they shine in your eyes, you are in love with them"

"The reflection of love is linked with the reflection of hearts"

"Love creates excitement between the hearts of people who are in love"

"Trust is when we feel that they are with us"

"The equation of love is love plus love equals love"

"When listening to them becomes the gain of life, they are quite special for you"

"Night is for love, relationship, and expression"

"When you are with them, you feel something special, and you want to stay in those feelings, you are in love"

"The success and sustainability of love show people's fortune"

"Love matters are dealt with by the heart"

"When you love someone, you also love yourself"

"When you feel that you can touch the sky and fly if they are with you, you are in love"

"When it is dark and they are around you, you can feel them from your heart and see them through its eyes"

"Child-to-parent attachment improves parents' emotional well-being"

"Love comes suddenly, but it does not go away suddenly"

"Love connects to people's hearts"

"When the time moves so fast while they are with you, and it stops when you are eager to meet with them, you are in love"

"Love can't sustain between people without the existence of trust"

"Love brightens when lovers are satisfied"

"Hearts start talking when people fall in love"

"Love is like two eyes that look for one another"

"When you see your reflection in your partner, your relationship becomes two souls, one reflection"

"Love, care, and respect are intertwined in people's relationships"

"When their one smile makes you forget all your worries at a time, you are in love with them"

"Love is the light in a dark night"

"People who are in love, their hearts are bigger than the universe"

"Love is challenging which comes with hopes and colorful dreams"

"Distance further connects two people who love each other"

"True lovers reflect each other"

"Love is like two hands in which both need each other"

"Love is a hidden treasure which becomes a fortune for fewer people"

"Love brightens when lovers are unified"

"Hearts talk when people love each other"

"When you direct all your wishes toward them, you are in love with them"

"When you see your reflection in their eyes and feel it, they are in love with you"

"Love is a thirst of hearts"

"The heart feels beyond the universe"

"Independence is a pride which gives citizens liberty, motivates them, and helps strengthen their abilities to progress and succeed in society"

"Love shines when lovers excite each other"

"When you cannot control your heart from thinking about them, you are in love with them"

"When the heart grows in love, people feel they concur with their life"

"The excitement of hearts and silence of faces are an indication of love"

"Love grows when the thirst of love is linked with the heart"

"Love grows when each word becomes precious, and each movement becomes charming"

"Love grows when you gift them your heart"

"Love grows when their happiness makes you happy"

"Trust is when they hold your hands and don't know where you go but smile because they are with you"

"Love doesn't interpret anything wrong in them"

"When all their words and actions feel exciting and pleasant to you, you are in love"

"Love is a strength which transforms people's lives"

"When the song of love is written by the heart and sung by eyes, you are in love"

"Success in love is an invaluable blessing for people, which can't be taken for granted"

"Trust is when the heart accepts their words"

"You may not know whom you love, but you need to know how you will love them"

"The heart's nature is to love others and it gets sick when it doesn't experience it"

"Sometimes love doesn't need any words because faces tell the story of what the hearts feel"

"The eyes tell what the hearts hide in love"

"The face of love stays in the heart and reflects through the eyes"

"People who love each other don't talk but their hearts talk between them, and they send and receive messages between them"

"When your emotions strongly connect you with them and you listen more than you talk, you are in love"

"Love is hidden in the heart which shows through people's actions and expressions"

"A smile reflects what you feel in your heart about them whom you love"

"The motivation for love arises when you feel them in your heart"

"Love is forgetting the self but remembering them"

"A positive silence between people shows that their feelings are talking, and they are emotionally connected"

"Love creates connections between eyes and heart and people can read it"

"The pleasant smile of both partners is the solution of many relationship problems for them"

"Blessed hearts are blessed with love"

"When their talk promotes your listening and their silence grows your emotions, you are in love"

"Love doesn't lie because people can't hide it"

"When their face becomes your universe, you are in love"

"The face of love is the face of the heart"

"Trust is deeper than an ocean in love"

"Love is the nature of people's hearts"

"The smile of love is the smile of the heart"

"The acceptance of love is the acceptance of hearts between people"

"One of the qualities of love is that it brings people closer together"

"Life ends when love disappears from the universe"

"The heart is deep in feeling something, whereas the mind is deep in thinking something"

"When they talk, you listen, and when you don't talk, you may listen to them"

"True love is a quality of good hearts"

"True hearts don't lie and they bring people together"

"Love is the nature of the heart"

"Love is the face of the heart"

"Love and the heart are deep and complex"

"Only important things touch the heart"

"Love uncovers the qualities of the heart"

"When people are in love, they don't see others"

"People experience love when the heart feels different about a person"

"A person whom you love becomes the entire universe"

"People become a reflection of each other in love"

"Love is linked in people's heart and face"

"The face of love locates in the eyes of lovers"

"Love is a priceless gift for the heart"

"People become humble and genuine before the one whom they love"

"Love is the beauty of the heart"

"The proximity between two hearts forms a love relationship"

"The fragrance of love centers in the heart"

"Love is an expansion of the heart for others"

"Love promotes sensitivity between people"

"Love is a destination of the heart"

"The sweetness of the heart reflects when people love others"

"You are nothing and they are everything in love"

"There is no negativity in love because love promotes positivity"

"When two people love one another, their two souls become a reflection"

"Love and intimacy are deeper than an ocean"

"Love and intimacy are complex and intertwined"

"Love grows emotional proximity between people"

"People's physical attachments are the result of their emotional proximity"

"People's love is a blessing for any heart"

"Trust brings people closer to one another"

"When you have nothing to remember except them, you are in love"

"Intimacy is intentional, whereas love is sudden"

"Love and intimacy are two pillars of a healthy relationship"

"Intimacy has various degrees and forms"

"The nature and meaning of intimacy vary among people"

"Intimacy between people evolves and changes over time"

"Love is a journey that doesn't have any destination"

"Love finds the heart when people are in love"

"Trust is when their everything becomes acceptable"

"Trust is when the heart feels everything right"

"Trust is when they say something and you agree without saying anything"

"Trust prevents people from having doubts and conflicts"

"Intimacy is a process which grows trust and affection in relationships"

"The process of intimacy is complex and ongoing"

"The face is a driving force of love"

"Love is when the heart connects with the face"

"Love is when they stay quiet and you hope to hear them"

"Love is when you want to see them even when they don't talk to you"

"Love controls the heart when people are in love"

"Love shapes the thinking of the heart"

"Love is what you feel and experience in yourself about the other person"

"Loving self and others are intertwined"

"Love is a reflection of people's feelings for one another"

"When people can't control their feelings and emotions about another person, they are in love"

"Love is an intensive emotional state that people experience"

"Prayer of love is the prayer of the heart"

"Pure people love purely"

"Love is a celebration of the heart"

"Only blessed hearts can absorb love and its blessings"

"Love is the life of the heart"

"Love makes two souls one reflection"

"Love is the dearest thing in this world"

"Love to love makes love relationships"

"When they talk and you listen, you don't want to talk but listen, you are in love with them"

"Intimacy grows with trust and companionship"

"Love and relationships with people grow together"

"The heart understands the feelings of love with others"

"The feeling of love is created in the heart"

"The nature of the heart is purity and love"

"The complexity of the heart is revealed when people love others"

"Sometimes love doesn't need an explanation, you show them your face and they will understand it"

"Love is the wealth and strength of the heart"

"Love is easy to feel but it is difficult to understand"

"Eyes learn about others' beauty and people's heart interprets it"

"The most beautiful experience of the heart is to love someone"

"Love has multiple layers that people experience over time"

"Love gives a purpose and motivation of life to people"

"The relevance of love is linked with the person who you love"

"Love is wealth that can't be measured"

"Love is restless and exhausting"

"Love motivates the heart to love others"

"The victory of love is when both partners love each other"

"The tragedy of love is when one person loves and the other doesn't"

"The heart feels the best for people when it experiences love"

"Love is when they are tired of talking and you want to hear them more"

"The heart is a reflection of love"

"The excitement of love is linked with those who you love"

"When your heart accepts them without any doubts, you are in love with them"

"The softness of the heart uncovers when people are in love"

"Love brightens the heart and soul"

"When people are in love, everything becomes irrelevant to them except one person whom they love"

"Love doesn't become fair because both partners can't love each other in the same way and degree"

"The symbol of love is the person whom you love"

"I make you happy to feel happy because I love you"

"When people feel they are flying in the sky without wings, they are in love"

"Love is like a quiet ocean"

"Love grows the self-esteem of both partners who are in love with each other"

"Love gets old but it doesn't die"

"Love gives you eyes that only see the person whom you love"

"The person whom you love is the love of your heart"

"Love and the heart have the same nature"

"Love satisfies people and their hearts"

"Love is an exciting but peaceful journey of two people"

"Hearts don't like when people stop them from loving others"

"People trust in those whom they love"

"Love enlightens the heart and soul"

"Intimacy helps people to grow sustainable relationships"

"Trust is like giving yourself for nothing"

"Love is the deepest human emotion"

"Love is the life of the heart"

"Love creates beauty in the heart"

"Love is the reflection of the heart"

"Love teaches people important lessons of life"

"When they are happy with me from their heart, I feel successful in love"

"People's thinking and feelings evolve when they love others"

"Love doesn't have any secret because it happens naturally"

"Love is successful when both partners are happy with each other"

"Love is the closeness of two hearts"

"Intimacy fosters an understanding of the relationship between people"

"Though you are two souls, you can make yourself one reflection of them"

"The heart creates feelings of love for others which reflect on people's face"

"Love of people determines the love of life for individuals"

"Peoples' face is the mirror of their heart"

Family and Relationships

"The fragrance of an attachment doesn't disappear; people feel it whenever they need it"

"Siblings mentor and educate each other every day, and parents need to promote such practices"

"Parenting is one of the most challenging but rewarding roles in society, and one smile of a child changes how parents feel about it"

"When children smile and parents feel pride, parents experience a great degree of well-being and happiness"

"Siblings' positive attachments show long-term positive outcomes for them"

"Investments in building relationships show lifelong returns"

"There is no scale in the world which can measure a mother's love for her child"

"Siblings become enduring support and resources for each other"

"The sensation of life is embedded in people's relationships"

"Love and relationships substantiate each other"

"Father is a shadow for children in tough situations"

"Fatherhood shows hard work, commitment, and toughness"

"Relationships are sustained when hearts are connected and emotionally closer to one another"

"Love is a useful tool to build healthy relationships"

"Siblings and friends share quite similar qualities"

"Mothers signify the sincerest relationship with their children"

"Grandparents have priceless wisdom for their children and grandchildren"

"A mother's love for her child is the mother of all love"

"Siblings are the best friends and mentors of each other"

"Grandparents have priceless wisdom"

"Relationships become meaningless without love and compassion between people"

"A mother is a symbol of patience, love, and compassion"

"Parents are the strongest shelter for children, they never collapse for them"

"A father shows commitment and resilience for his children, he never get tired of hardships"

"Children's presence brings joy and happiness for their parents and increases their motivation"

"Children's company is a unique blessing for their parents"

"Parents gain strength and energy when they hug their children"

"The most sustainable love is a mother's love for her children"

"Trust is when you sleep in their lap and not worry about getting up because you know they take care of you"

"Motherhood promotes courage and patience"

"Motherhood is beyond hard work and hardships"

"Children's appreciation for their parents is the ultimate source of motivation for them"

"The most energetic source for parents is when they watch their children be happy and joyful"

"People's personal happiness is linked with those who are associated with them by any means"

"True friends are a lifelong blessing for people"

"Children show their reflection and the reflection of their primary caregiver"

"Attachments between people are a core element for sustaining positive relationships over time"

"Children's smiles makes their parents stronger and motivated"

"Trust is when you are hungry but still happy because you know food will be given to you"

"Home is a symbol of harmony, protection, and safety"

"Trust is when you know they hold your hand and won't leave you even if it could cost them their life"

"Trust is like sleeping in a dense jungle without worrying because you know they are watching you"

"Siblings' conflict becomes a useful learning experience for them when it is dealt with positively by them and their elders"

"Parents' sensitivity to their children's needs is crucial for their optimal development"

"When children connect with their grandparents, they receive invaluable and enduring social and emotional support"

"The authenticity of the heart creates closeness between people and brings them together"

"Trust builds when children know their parents are doing everything for them during the time when they need it"

"Investments are in building positive parent-child relationships, they produce valuable returns for their whole lives"

"Positive parent-child relationships are a determinant of healthy children, parents, and family functioning"

"Parent-child healthy relationships are a symbol of trust for others"

"Children's growth is linked with parents' motivation to grow and develop them"

"Parents and children are life motivation and a source of development for each other"

"Siblings foster a mentoring process for each other"

"The most impactful male role model for children is their father"

"The one thing which is uncountable is a mother's love for her children"

"Trust repairs and maintains challenging relationships"

"People who like each other can stand together"

"Trust is when you are ready to give your life for them and stay satisfied"

"Women's intimacy is central to successful and sustainable couple and family relationships"

"Parents are a symbol of love for society"

"Excessive interference of money in relationships makes them unhealthy"

"Women have natural characteristics to form and maintain healthy and nurturing relationships"

"Love situates at the center of people and relationships"

"Trust remains a stronger factor in parent-child relationships when children become adults"

"Women play integral roles in growing and sustaining population globally"

"Trust is when you give everything without asking any questions"

"People who trust each other don't see the drawbacks of their relationship"

"The cost of trust is hard work and commitment"

"When people are satisfied with themselves, they are satisfied with the world"

"Active listening is a foundation of healthy relationships"

"Intimacy takes many faces and forms"

"Trust is when you accept all their actions"

"Trust teaches patience and persistence"

"The ultimate goal of enduring relationships is building trust"

"The essence of life is in good feelings about self and others"

"Pure hearts make successful relationships"

"The success of life is in sharing and making connections"

"The degree of satisfaction makes life calm and happy"

"Siblings are an enduring asset of life"

"People are satisfied when they do what they want"

"Marriage increases the resilience of partners"

"When people face problems together, they develop stronger relationships"

"Enduring relationships are trustworthy and respectful"

"Humbleness and patience prevent people from anger and resentment"

"Trust is when you follow them without thinking about any consequences"

"The feeling of loneliness is more damaging for people than the actual loneliness"

"Parent-child healthy conversations show the degree and nature of their relationship"

"Parents' typical conversations with children even contain substantial pieces of advice for them"

"Raising children and making them productive citizens is the greatest achievement of life for parents"

"When relationships evolve, they become healthy and successful"

"Healthy parent-child conversations contain substantial benefits for both"

"Parent-child attachment remains quite stable over the course of life once they are developed"

"Parents stand tall like mountains despite all hardships due to their children's success"

"Acceptance and humbleness resolve many problems between people"

"The alignment between children's eyes and face when they smile shows parents' success"

"Parents' love is a constant blessing for children"

"People's healthy relationships with others create a legacy for them"

"Happiness and joy are uncovered when people build healthy relationships with others"

"When parents develop positive attachments with their children, their children sleep well"

"Positive relationships increase people's resilience in tough situations"

"Youth is like a short but pleasant dream"

"People with positive energies are good for themselves who also boost others' positive thoughts and emotions"

"The mind recalls childhood memories anytime because these memories have a strong impact on it"

"Positive family relationships make family members strong and resilient"

"Positivity is a unique source which energizes and motivates people"

"Families are essential for the success of the individual, community, and society"

"Healthy relationships show resilience in hardships"

"Siblings improve each other's communication skills"

"Happiness is an interrelated and multifaceted phenomenon"

"A mother is a symbol of softness and love"

"Parents are the face of life"

"Children are life motivation for those who need it"

"Contemporary families are complex and evolving"

"There is no one simple way to understand a family's experiences"

"Each family is unique and does not follow straightforward rules"

"Families are the engine of a prosperous society"

Friendship and Society

"People's attitudes and characters are shaped by their country and its historical context"

"The friends of the heart are those whom you love"

"When people honor themselves, they honor others as well"

"Sustainability is preserving resources and simultaneously discovering new resources for addressing current and future needs"

"Economies become self-sufficient and sustainable when people work hard and devote their lives for the country"

"The idea of friendship is living together without showing any formalities"

"Life is boring without any hardships"

"Good friends support people in pursuing their positive dreams"

"Tough situations teach people important lessons and make them stronger"

"Friends stay in the heart and influence the mind"

"Friends shape people's thinking and attitudes toward others and oneself"

"Positive friendship forms and promotes people's constructive goals"

"Sincere friends are like trees who tolerate all types of weather but still stand together"

"Friendship is a symbol of love and companionship"

"Friends create love and love creates friends"

"Trust is like following them with closed eyes and not stopping until they say so"

"Life is a race during which you can't go backward"

"The success of people's lives is in facing conflicts constructively and finding solutions to deal with them rather than ignoring or avoiding them"

"Sincere friends build trust and become valuable assets"

"People's personal experiences make them sensitive to others' experiences"

"Life is like a race during which you can't stop"

"When people deal with conflicts in constructive ways, they learn invaluable life skills"

"The wealth of knowledge grows when you distribute it among people"

"Humans and education are the most useful and sustainable resources for contemporary societies"

"Friends are characters who take various roles to help and support each other in a friendship"

"Constructive engagement decreases conflicts"

"All societies are complex, groups are diverse, and families are unique"

"Successful societies create supportive environments for their citizens and provide them with relevant and valuable opportunities according to their educational levels and skills"

"Successful societies form and prioritize ethical standards for their citizens"

"Aging is a blessing and not a stigma"

"Time becomes the worst enemy of those who don't care about it"

"Friends are a treasure that is easy to find but difficult to preserve"

"One independence exists at the societal level, whereas the other independence lies in people; both need to be encouraged and fostered"

"Different forms of love and relationship are imperative for the smooth functioning and success of society"

"When they meet with you after a while, and you still find your connection with them, they are your friends"

"Your food becomes more delicious when you think about others who don't have any"

"The progress of any society is in its people's hands"

"Independence saves lives, frees people from slavery, and increases their potential to a great level"

"Wiseness doesn't depend on age because it relates to people's wisdom"

"The secret of life is hidden in humans' experiences"

"Good memories provide people with positive connections with the past and motivation for the future"

"Independence is a unique blessing that all citizens of society feel to an extent, and this feeling doesn't end but grows over time"

"Trust in a relationship is like water for life"

"Trust develops when there are no doubts between people"

"People become great when they understand others' feelings"

"All areas of society are equally important for its growth and development"

"Relationships situate at the center of people's lives"

"Sustainable relationships are a success of people in contemporary societies"

"Politeness is the core element in initiating healthy interactions with others"

"People reveal their emotions when they talk to others"

"Self-control protects individuals from many troubles and makes them succeed in life"

"Successful youth become proactive, persistent, and patient"

"Aging populations need additional support from society to expand opportunities and minimize challenges for themselves"

"When people work together with a learning attitude, they teach and learn from one another"

"Support, enthusiasm, and entertainment are the hallmark of friendship"

"Life becomes more pleasant for people when they experience the beauty of it"

"Successful nations are proactive in making rules and implementing them"

"Money is a symbol of respect in a social world"

"Money can't buy good characters of people"

"Friendship grows with trust and companionship"

"Motivation and appreciation are essential for promoting people's work"

"Intimacy is intentional, whereas love is sudden"

"Love and intimacy are two pillars of healthy relationships"

"Intimacy has various degrees and forms"

"The nature and meaning of intimacy varies among people"

"Intimacy between people evolves and changes over time"

"Friendship is meaningless without trust"

"Trust is the main pillar on which friendship stands successfully"

"Friendship promotes quality of life"

"Feelings and emotions have their own language"

"Healthy friendship offers more rewards than costs"

"People's love and passion for their country substantiate institutional efforts which are made for the betterment of the country"

"All actors are equally important who work together to make their country succeed"

"Positive friendship provides people with a good foundation for learning and development"

"Friendship has a great deal of benefits for all partners"

"Real-life experiences expand people's knowledge that they learn in any setting"

"Intimacy is a process of relationship development with people"

"Intimacy creates stability in a relationship"

"Intimacy is an essential element of friendship"

"Friendship is about building intimacy in relationships"

"One way to deal with hardships is to look at others' struggles"

"There is nothing like people's real-life experiences and the lessons they learn from them"

"Biases and prejudice become irrelevant in a friend relationship"

"Sustainable efforts bring tough situations for people but they address people's important problems on a long-term basis"

"Constructive ways to deal with hardships are positive learning experiences for people"

"Hardships make people tough and resilient"

"People's wealth is a product of their internal and external sources and qualities"

"Trust is a process of uncovering people's individual self"

"Intimacy and trust are intertwined in a love relationship"

"Holding hands is a sign of trust between people"

"Dance brings partners closer to one another and promotes intimacy between them"

"Both partners create intimacy in their relationship because intimacy is bidirectional"

"Trust makes people fearless"

"Intimacy brings two hearts closer to one another"

"Intimacy doesn't have any meaning because people create it's meaning"

"Care is an essential aspect of building love relationships"

"Self-reflection promotes positive relationships between people"

"Knowledge, experience, and social status are an important symbol of authority among people"

"Friendship is an essential aspect of a happy life, particularly for those who need it"

"Friendship teaches people how to practice intimacy"

"True friendship grows from the heart"

"Language and manners can either break or strengthen relationships between people"

"Friendship is a lifelong resource for people"

"Friendship is a symbol of love and compassion"

"Friendship is a lifelong blessing"

"Friendship is a beautiful and lifelong blessing"

"Friendship builds naturally as it requires time"

"Friendship is the core of the human experience"

"Friendship needs substantial investments which pay off over time"

"Friends' hearts are pure for each other"

"Friends are priceless gifts for people"

Science and Education

"Societies need growth and change with a certain degree of stability"

"The meaning of life is embedded in its discovery and experience"

"People's desires can't be fulfilled because they evolve over time"

"The evolution of mind is beyond humans' thinking"

"Knowledge is a tool which sharpens over time when we use it"

"Educators are the engine of a successful society, whereas society determines the degree of their functionality"

"People use their mind to gain education and education grows people's mind"

"Education and educators are essential sources for society to grow and foster sustainable efforts and actions"

"Education is a fundamental resource of educated people"

"Questions promote discovery and exploration"

"Critical thinking fosters when people ask questions"

"Educators and the education system are a reflection of any society"

"One of the most sustainable resources on the earth is education"

"Educators are an essential element of successful and sustainable societies"

"The relevance increases the rigor of assessments"

"Teachers' appreciation is a priceless prize for their students"

"Teachers' encouragement is a tool of success for students"

"Relaxation is a prize of hard work"

"Theories are rigorous assessment tools"

"Theories connect research and assessment"

"Theories are useful assessment frameworks"

"Theories examine real-life situations and provide substantial guidance"

"Science and technology are the fundamental pillars of contemporary societies"

"Day and night substantiate each other to support human life"

"The space in the heart is like the space in the universe"

"The heart, mind, and universe share similar qualities"

"People's internal conflict is more harmful for them than external problems until it is effectively resolved"

"Resolution lies in conflict which is uncovered through mutual support and a reflective process"

"Conflict resolution requires reflection, responsibility, and reciprocity"

"Critical thinking and observation are crucial elements for the production of new knowledge"

"Successful societies promote critical thinking and decision-making among their citizens"

"Rigor is embedded in the cultural lens of assessments"

"It is research which makes things real that initially feel unreal"

"Constructive listening and speaking increase people's knowledge"

"Critical thinking and observation are crucial for the production of new knowledge"

"Contemporary assessments need relevance and generalizability"

"Every research study is important and supports the other"

"People's interest in specific areas promotes discovery and innovation in those areas"

"Human thinking evolves when people learn to think"

"Though the mind is rational and the heart is emotional, they are intertwined"

"Existing assessments need to be examined through a cultural lens, whereas new assessments need cultural accountability"

"Hard work, efficiency, and consistency are important determinants of people's success"

"Research is a scientific and systematic but reflective process"

"Assessments need a cultural lens to become inclusive and relevant"

"The human imagination is an important element of science"

"Humans' thinking is an essential source for knowledge creation for them"

"The heart and mind are the strength of this universe"

"The mind creates the power of thinking"

"The legacy of knowledge is promoted by people's fame"

"The awareness of life is the success of humans"

"Time is a friend of successful people"

"Time hurts those who hurt it"

"Questioning prepares people intellectually"

"Knowledge doesn't have any limits"

"Knowledge is a tool which sharpens with time"

"The philosophy of time is relevant with human life"

"The reflection of self promotes intellect among people"

"Successful people have control over their heart and mind"

"Unhealthy self is the worst enemy of people"

"People can't undo their life because of time"

"Life is colorful with the dynamic nature of time"

"The risk is an element of success"

"Strong mind and heart open up opportunities and minimize vulnerabilities"

"Teaching is a reflective and transformative process of learning"

"The complexity of humans reflects through their lives"

"The success of individuals is the success of society"

"Life is based on counted breathing"

"The resolution of life lies in optimism"

"The philosophy of life lies in humans' experiences"

"Human thinking is a driving force in decision making"

"When people learn to reflect, they become intellectual"

"People can't buy peace of heart"

"Successful people are calm, consistent, and creative"

"Creativity is a core basis for a progressive society"

"The hunger of knowledge promotes education among people"

"People's love for knowledge is the key to their success in education"

"Science and knowledge protect human life"

"Science and human life are interdependent"

"Rigor and context make assessments accurate and meaningful"

"Education is one of the fundamental and strongest pillars of societies"

"Rigor is linked with an understanding of the context for conducting assessments"

"Creative minds bring substantial shifts in society"

"Creative minds' mentoring is essential for progressive societies"

"Life ends when time becomes irrelevant"

"When people respect time, they become successful"

"Schools are one of the strongest pillars of society"

"The distribution of knowledge is the distribution of success and value among others"

"The competence of people's knowledge is uncovered when they practice it"

"Schools are a sustainable resource for sustainable societies"

"Knowledge makes people humble and calm"

"Life is a race with time in which time always wins"

"Time can become the best friend or the worst enemy"

"Rigor is embedded in the cultural lens of assessments"

"Research designs determine the rigor of scientific research"

"Theories provide a conceptual framework, whereas research designs offer an empirical framework to a study"

"Education is wealth that people can earn anytime"

"Critical thinking and observation are fundamentals for self-reflection"

"Imagination, observation, and empirical testing are key elements for the advancement of science"

"Critical thinking and observation are crucial for the production of new knowledge"

"Critical thinking is promoted in higher education and education fosters critical thinking among people"

"Educators are the ambassadors of education"

"Research is a light to find something which hides in the dark"

"Research is a combination of known and unknown facts"

"There is nothing but reflexivity which disentangles our subjectivity from the objective truth"

"Research is a hope for a prosperous world"

"Research becomes like a horrible dream which keeps scaring us until we master it"

"Research is not entirely about what we find, but is more about how we find it"

"The value of work determines its significance for society"

"Research demands passion and patience"

"The science of research is in the process of doing it"

"Rigor and reflexivity are two equally important dimensions of scientific research"

"Learning grows humans' knowledge beyond educational limits"

"Questions open ways for exploration and discovery"

"Knowledge is a blessing which doesn't end in life"

"Happiness grows when people like themselves"

"The secret of knowledge is embedded in learning"

"Human experiences grow scientific knowledge"

"Life is a complex question which doesn't have simple answers"

"The most wonderful blessing of life is life itself"

"Hard work creates its own luck"

"The self is deeper than the ocean"

"Dreams drive their reality"

"Fame is priceless and pleasant"

"Life is a short but pleasant dream"

"Life shows in every breath you take"

"A certain degree of dependency on others shows a sign of association with them"

"Life is a continuous reflective process"

"People reflect on their life when they don't have much time"

"The nature of this universe reflects from humans' experiences"

"Education is a sustainable resource for those who need it"

"Dreams are a motivation to achieve life goals"

"Patience and persistence can beat any adversity"

"Trust and good manners make people valuable among others"

"Everyone likes that person who likes themselves"

"Morning is the hope of life"

"Life needs immediate but wise decisions on time to succeed"

"Peoples' dreams become roadmaps for them in their life"

"The feeling of early morning refreshes the mind"

"Peoples' beliefs can defeat their actions"

"The freshness of morning is the peace of mind"

Leadership and Culture

"Food sharing creates love and connections between people"

"Leaders have patience and a soft heart for their nation"

"Cultural sustainability is linked with people's healthy relationships"

"Global engagement benefits contemporary societies where there is self-sufficiency in core areas of the economy"

"Cultural traditions need to be adaptive to preserve the culture and ensure it's sustainability"

"When existing and new cultural traditions are interesting, people take part in it and carry them"

"Cultural flexibility ensures it's sustainability"

"Interesting, relevant, and engaged cultural traditions are enduring and adaptable"

"When leadership becomes charismatic, people fall in love with their leaders"

"Leaders have hidden strengths which attract people toward them"

"Leaders' vision and clarity of thoughts attract people toward them"

"Leaders give hope and optimism to their followers"

"Leaders always encourage their followers to do better in life"

"Favorite foods bring positive changes in people's moods"

"Music is adaptive in nature, which represents people's tastes over time"

"People are a driving force who bring changes in music over time"

"When people are connected with their food, traditions, and language, they preserve their culture"

"The preservation of culture is essential for a group existence in society"

"Music is a good way to leave an enduring legacy behind you"

"Music creates memories and brings people together"

"Food plays an important role in establishing cultural traditions"

"Leaders stay in people's eyes and live in their hearts"

"Singing entertains the body and soothes the soul"

"Dance promotes pride and humbleness"

"People's beliefs are stronger than their actions because they influence both people's actions and outcomes associated with them"

"Dance is an important source of deep relaxation and happiness"

"Leaders stay alive for their followers"

"The legacy of leaders is their leadership qualities"

"True leaders build trust among their followers through their actions"

"Dance demonstrates the beauty of life before people"

"Dance captures the movements of life"

"Modern businesses prioritize, support, and facilitate their consumers"

"People ensure cultural sustainability by preserving their culture"

"Successful leadership is holistic and people centered"

"Positive gestures are fundamental to healthy relationships"

"Words are expressions of people's thoughts"

"Flowers buffer against conflicts and promote love between people"

"People can't control their heart to love true leaders"

"Leaders create charisma among their followers"

"Leaders are brave and resilient who neither get scared nor tired from any tough situation"

"Leaders give priority to their nation's interest over their own benefits"

"Leaders' words promote reflection and critical thinking among their people"

"Citizens find true leaders honest and authentic"

"Leaders' top priority is their country and its citizens"

"Pictures tell life stories and share pleasant memories"

"Leaders' primary wealth is their country's citizens"

"Ethical standards give people internal and external control in different domains of their life"

"When leaders promote and demonstrate ethics, people respect and follow them"

"Ethics and reflection transform the lives of leaders and their followers"

"Cooking and sharing traditional food are ways to sustain a culture"

"There are important distinctions between leaders and managers that organizations need to consider for better functioning"

"A vision provides continuity to organizations"

"Gratitude and appreciation connect people together and promote positive feelings between them"

"The relevance of leaders' visions promotes the leadership among people and attracts them toward leaders"

"Leaders make their own benefits irrelevant and people's benefits and welfare the most relevant to them"

"Leaders are transformative in all aspects of their life, which also reflects among their people"

"Music is a source of individual and collective entertainment"

"When people receive a message in their heart that their leaders are sincere for them and their nation, they start following them"

"A cultural evolution is supported by people and society"

"Cultures have hidden aspects and strengths for people"

"Food is a source of cultural connections and sharing between people"

"Food and music are two important elements of cultural sustainability"

"Cultural food and music make people happy when they are alone"

"When people promote cultural food and music, they preserve their culture"

"Music and food create cultural excitement"

"Food and music create meaningful cultural memories"

"Food recalls pleasantness and creates excitement among people"

"Cultural food creates a sense of belonging among people"

"Cultural food and music are essential resources to keep people connected with it"

"Shared food creates a meaning between people"

"Leaders live in the hearts of people and receive unconditional love from them"

"Visionary leaders change people's mind and heart"

"Pleasant music creates happy and strong memories"

"When leaders walk, they talk even though they stay quiet"

"Followers love everything that their leader does"

"Leaders' smiles give energy to their followers"

"Food becomes a source of initiating healthy relationships"

"Leaders' body language conveys many important messages to their followers"

"Shared singing promotes intimacy between partners"

"True leaders are a driving force of people's minds and hearts"

"The feelings of a country's independence create pride among its people"

"Leaders don't insist anyone follow them, people follow them due to their charismatic personality"

"Dance is a practice of spirituality"

"Dance is a blessing for the body and soul"

Spirituality and Compassion

"Love and compassion with people is the essence of life"

"Spirituality addresses all aspects of people's life and guides them accordingly"

"Spirituality is staying happy in all conditions"

"Spirituality is about learning the depth of our heart"

"When the peace of the heart reflects on the face, the signs of spirituality grow"

"Spirituality promotes a strong connection between body and soul"

"Spirituality promotes love and trust"

"When people feel their soul, they become spiritual"

"Spirituality is discovering the trust of heart and soul"

"Compassion benefits people and society"

"Compassion improves self and others' well-being"

"Spirituality is informed by its relevant religion"

"Spirituality is an individual's practice in a unique manner"

"When people become spiritual, their body and heart calm down and relax"

"Patience is the best weapon against evils"

"Spirituality is beyond the thinking of the mind"

"The awareness of self and an understanding of others is spirituality"

"Spirituality promotes purity in all aspects of people's life"

"Good hearts promote sacrifice for others"

"The purity of the heart forms healthy relationships"

"Children are spiritual in nature and become role models for others who practice spirituality"

"Spirituality is thanking those that you have and those that you don't have"

"People discover life when they love others"

"The body and soul purify each other when people become spiritual"

"The heart brightens and the soul enlightens when spirituality grows"

"When the body connects with the heart and soul, people become spiritual"

"Spirituality grows positive connections between people and with those who they don't see"

"People uniquely experience, learn, and practice spirituality"

"When the self is devoted to others, the signs of spirituality grow"

"Listening, actions, and intentions are fundamental elements of spirituality"

"Spirituality grows and promotes harmony in people's lives and in the lives of others"

"Spirituality is revealing the purity of the heart for others"

"Spirituality encourages the discovery of soul through the purity of the heart"

"Spirituality is searching for oneself"

"Love of people is the basis of spirituality"

"Spirituality is giving yourself and taking them"

"Spirituality builds strong trust in those who we connect with"

"The spiritual soul recognizes its origin"

"Spirituality is the peace of heart, mind, and soul"

"People experience spirituality when they love everyone and don't hate"

"Spirituality creates and builds people's connections with those who they don't see"

"Spirituality grows when people's hearts talks to them"

"The success of hearts is in loving others"

"Spirituality is about giving your heart and taking their trust"

"The blessings of spirituality grow with people's personal and interpersonal qualities"

"Spirituality addresses all aspects of people's life and guides them accordingly"

"Spirituality awakens the heart, enlightens the soul, and purifies the body"

"The evolution of the heart and soul is spirituality"

"Spirituality is a buffer against life stressors"

"Spirituality builds trust in oneself and in those who grow people's spirituality"

"Spirituality takes people's humbleness, compassion, and sense of sacrifice to a high degree"

"The discovery of soul and heart is spirituality"

"Spirituality is the purity of heart and soul"

"Spirituality is the blessing of the heart"

"People experience spirituality when they are humble, forgiving, and compassionate"

"Spirituality is raising the body and soul in a positive manner"

"The nature of the heart is to love oneself and others who are around you"

"Spirituality expands the heart and purifies the soul"

"The connection between heart and soul grows spirituality"

"Spirituality is the literacy of the heart"

"Listening creates opportunities for people to learn, understand, and reflect"

"Intentions are more valuable and important than actions in spirituality because they drive people's action"

"Listening, respect, and responsiveness are essential elements of spirituality"

"Spiritual people find their peace in spirituality"

"Passion to help and compassion for others are essential to leave a valuable legacy"

"When people help others, they spiritually grow themselves"

"When you don't want to talk just because it takes time away from listening to them, they become special for you"

"The signs of spirituality grow when they talk and you listen"

"The world is grounded in love and compassion between people"

"The soul and heart grow healthy when people become spiritual"

"Purity of heart is an essential condition for loving others"

"Spirituality is the richness of the heart"

"Spirituality is different from religion but it is embedded in religion"

"Spirituality gives life to the heart"

"The qualities of the heart are revealed when people become spiritual"

"The heart needs training, mentoring, and connection to grow spiritually"

"Spirituality creates peace, contentment, and satisfaction for people"

"Searching for self and understanding others is spirituality"

"Spirituality is forgetting oneself and finding them"

"People's hearts evolve when they experience spirituality"

"People become spiritual when they feel others' worries"

"People forget self-worries when they become spiritual"

"Spirituality widens the heart and purifies the soul"

"Love and spirituality are natural aspects of people"

"Spirituality discovers the nature of the soul"

"Spirituality and love are intertwined, which are inherited in people"

"When people's hearts and souls practice spirituality, they become spiritual"

"The soul experiences its nature in spirituality"

"The practice and meaning of spirituality vary among people"

"Spirituality promotes harmony of the heart and mind"

"Spirituality benefits individuals and other people who are around them"

"Spirituality is finding a connection with them and maintaining it"

"Spirituality is about making connections with those who you don't see"

"Spirituality is about thinking about self and others"

"Spiritual people are full of hope and optimism"

"Compassion is an integral part of practicing spirituality"

"Spirituality is finding something that you don't know about"

"Patience is the practice of victorious people"

"Spirituality is building trust in them and holding it"

"Spirituality widens the heart and grows the soul"

"The discovery of self is spirituality"

"The calmness of heart shows signs of spirituality"

"The awareness of who you are is spirituality"

"Dance promotes a feeling of closeness in spirituality"

"People understand the meaning of dance in spirituality"

"Spirituality is people's love which gives life to the heart"

"Dance becomes meaningful in spirituality"

"The heart reads and the soul listens in spirituality"

"Spirituality removes darkness from the heart and brightens it"

"Spirituality gives life to the heart and soul"

"Spirituality is about reading the heart and understanding the soul"

"Spirituality is finding the heart and soul"

"Spirituality is revealing the secret of the heart and soul"

"Spirituality is delving into the heart and soul and discovering oneself"

"Spirituality is becoming thankful in every condition"

"There are no complaints in spirituality"

"The relaxation of heart and mind is spirituality"

"Spirituality is a treasure and the heart finds it"

"Spirituality is the wealth of the heart"

"Spirituality is a blessing of the heart"

"When people's hearts start talking to them, they become spiritual"

"Spirituality is balancing the needs of body and soul"

"The humbleness of the heart is spirituality"

"Spirituality is hope to live a purposeful life"

"Spirituality makes life meaningful for those who believe in it"

"Prayers are only one component of spirituality"

"Spirituality lightens the darkest hearts"

"The closeness of hearts brings bodies closer to one another"

"The discovery of heart and soul is spirituality"

"Spirituality is giving away everything and asking for nothing"

"The strength of spirituality is hidden in it"

"Spirituality opens the eyes of hearts"

"Self-reflection encourages people to explore their life"

"Practice of gratitude resolves many human problems"

"Gratitude grows a positive attitude toward life"

"The heart has hidden connections with divine forces"

"Spirituality is the happiness of the heart"

"Spirituality doesn't require any knowledge but it demands a pure heart"

"Spirituality requires hard work and sacrifice"

"Prayers give freshness to the body and soul"

"Death promotes the love of life"

"The practice of gratitude relaxes people and provides them with a peace of mind"

"Spirituality is talking to the heart"

"Spirituality is the prayer of the heart"

"Body and soul are in a conflict to conquer each other"

"When the desire of the heart is linked with peace of self and others, spirituality grows"

"The reflection of remaining life grows it for people in a positive manner"

Poetry and Writing

"Writing grows hope, happiness, and optimism"

"Life is like a race, people need to be energized, prepared, and keep running"

"Writing is the most durable and strongest weapon of all time"

"Poetry describes their face, beauty, and character"

"Poetry is an expression of what the heart feels about the one whom you love"

"Poetry is the language of love that is expressed in words and symbols"

"Poetry is a feeling of love between people"

"Writers of love experience, write, and practice love"

"Poetry contains several benefits for its readers and writers"

"Morning is a motivation for working hard, fulfilling responsibilities, and showing commitments to people"

"Nighttime book reading and writing are good for quality sleep"

"Book reading is training the mind to acquire knowledge"

"Writing is an expression of emotions"

"Poetry is a description of love and the person whom you love"

"Writing is a legacy of writers"

"Knowledge is a tool that sharpens with time"

"Writing promotes emotional well-being among writers"

"Writing of love goes beyond any limits because it is informed by the heart"

"Poetry is an affirmation of love"

"Eyes are the reflection of people's personality"

"Poetry is a pleasant form of writing"

"Poetry gives language and expression to a love relationship"

"Observation and critical thinking are essential elements for knowledge creation"

"Poetry connects heart and mind"

"Poetry helps people to understand, express, and control their emotions"

"Book reading sustains and fosters people's knowledge"

"Imagination and observation are key to science and the production of new knowledge"

"Morning is a symbol of hope, happiness, and happenings"

"When you can handle yourself, you can handle the world"

"People will believe in you when you believe in yourself"

"Poetry describes how the heart of one person feels love for the other"

"Morning and night are two fundamental pillars of a life that people need to hold and utilize to live a successful life"

"People who closely follow nature become more successful in their life"

"When people are excited to live their lives, they stay excited in tough situations"

"Dance and music improve the functionality of body and mind"

"Dance creates linkages between body, heart, and soul"

"Dance grows spirituality for those who believe in it"

"People's legacy is linked with their hard work, selflessness, and willing-ness to support others"

"Dance improves people's potential and brings it to a high degree"

"Writing is people's strongest tool"

"Poetry and writing create love and build positive relationships between people"

"Writing is an expression of self and our relationships with others"

"Poetry is an indirect mode of communication between partners"

"Writing and poetry express each other for readers"

"Poetry brings like-minded people together and creates a bond between them"

"Writing is a tool which does not get old but sharpens over time"

"Poetry is a written form of what the heart feels"

Conclusion

This is the very first book of its kind. The entire book is grounded and informed by unique statements (i.e., quotes). There are one thousand quotes in this book, which have not been said or written by anyone in the past. The author presented different aspects and ways of learning these quotes by offering an additional description for each quote, writing a story, providing an engaged activity, and including discussion questions to promote critical thinking, group engagement, and personal reflection about the quote.

This book applies to all groups of audiences including academic and nonacademic readers to learn these unique statements, which contain essential knowledge and information and further discover and explore them by applying these quotes to real-life situations. This book promotes an expansion of new knowledge such that readers can also write their own description of the quote based on their understanding of it. It also provides readers with opportunities to write and practice their own quotes.

This book can be used in a class for courses such as Quotes and Their Real-Life Application. Instructors can also use this book as a supplementary book in their courses related to love, relationships, culture, and society. There are many subtopics in this book which relate to the quotes. Hence, instructors can review this book and choose it for their course more appropriately. This book will promote creative work, group engagement, teamwork, critical thinking, self-reflection, and provide positive learning experiences to students and readers.

www.ingramcontent.com/pod-product-compliance
Lightning Source LLC
Chambersburg PA
CBHW071121280326
41935CB00010B/1082